DATE DUE

Freedom Summer

FREEDOM SUMMER

David Aretha

MORGAN REYNOLDS
PUBLISHING
Greensboro, North Carolina

THE CIVIL RIGHTS MOVEMENT

The Trial of the Scottsboro Boys

Marching in Birmingham

Selma and the Voting Rights Act

The Murder of Emmett Till

Freedom Summer

FREEDOM SUMMER
Copyright © 2008 by David Aretha

Library of Congress Cataloging-in-Publication Data

Aretha, David.
    Freedom Summer / by David Aretha. -- 1st ed.
        p. cm. -- (Civil rights series)
    Includes bibliographical references and index.
    ISBN-13: 978-1-59935-059-2
    ISBN-10: 1-59935-059-9
    1. African Americans--Civil rights--Mississippi--History--20th century-
-Juvenile literature. 2.   Mississippi Freedom Project--Juvenile literature. 3.
African Americans--Suffrage--Mississippi--History--20th century--Juvenile
literature. 4. Civil rights workers--Mississippi--History--20th century--Juvenile
literature. 5.   Civil rights movements--Mississippi--History--20th century--
Juvenile literature. 6.   Mississippi--Race relations--History--20th century--
Juvenile literature. I. Title.
    E185.93.M6A74 2007
    323.1196'073009046--dc22
                                                    2007023815

Printed in the United States of America
First Edition

Contents

Freedom Summer volunteer Jacob Blum hangs a voter registration sign in Mississippi.
(© *Herbert Randall, McCain Library & Archives, University of Southern Mississippi*)

one

Preface to a Long, Hot Summer

L ike every African American family in Mississippi in the early 1960s, the Chaneys, of Meridian, lived in the large, looming shadow of Jim Crow, the laws and regulations that relegated blacks to the status of second-class citizens. Ben toiled as a plasterer and Fannie a domestic servant, both for miniscule wages, and their five children seemed doomed to a life of hardship. Whites held all the power in Mississippi, and they intimidated blacks into submission. Yet James Chaney, the oldest of Ben and Fannie's children, dared to challenge the racial intolerance.

Shy and slightly built, Chaney was nonetheless determined to work for justice in Mississippi. As a high school student in 1959, he had refused to remove his NAACP (National Association for the Advancement of Colored People) button and was subsequently suspended. In 1963, when the Congress for Racial Equality (CORE) became active in Meridian, Chaney eagerly signed up. The following spring,

VOTER REGISTRATION

The struggle for freedom in Mississippi can only be won by a combination of action within the state and heightened awareness throughout the country of the need for enforcement of federal guarantees of basic human and political rights. While old and new federal laws support the right to vote, the government has not yet acted decisively to insure that all Americans can participate in governmental affairs.

In Mississippi, SNCC voter registration workers are operating in each Congressional district. Despite discriminatory voting laws and terrorism, voting workers and local Negroes have mobilized a state-wide organization for political action.

Freedom Registration has been established in most counties, with registration books closely resembling the official books of the state. The Freedom Registration Books are being used by the Freedom Democratic Party in its challenge of the all-white Democratic Party of Mississippi.

Finally, voter registration workers are assisting the campaigns of four Negroes running for Congressional office.

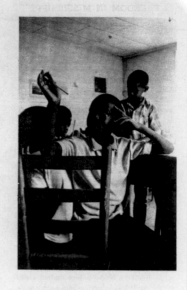

FREEDOM SCHOOLS

An integral part of SNCC's voter registration work throughout the rural South has been the development of young leadership. The Freedom School program was evolved to supply political education unavailable in Mississippi's public schools.

By mid-July, over thirty-five Freedom Schools had been established (three times the number expected) with an average daily enrollment across the state of 2,100. Instruction is highly individualized — each

This page from an SNCC pamphlet describes two of the main projects of the Freedom Summer: voter registration drives and freedom schools. *(Courtesy of Will D. Campbell Papers, McCain Library & Archives, University of Southern Mississippi)*

he was ready for a greater role when CORE and the Student Nonviolent Coordinating Committee (SNCC) organized the ambitious and dangerous Mississippi Summer Project, called Freedom Summer. Chaney would help black citizens register to vote.

"Mama," Chaney said, "I believe I done found an organization that I can be in and do something for myself and somebody else, too."

"Ain't you afraid of this?" his mother asked.

"Naw, Mama, that's what's the matter now—everybody's scared."

On June 21, the first day of summer, Chaney and two others volunteers he was driving with disappeared. The FBI spearheaded a statewide manhunt to find the missing young men and those responsible for the disappearance. The federal agents weren't especially interested in Chaney; blacks in Mississippi had been killed without much publicity for years. Instead, the FBI arrived on behalf of the other two missing volunteers—white Northerners of privileged background. The bodies of the three men were found on August 4. Each had been shot, and Chaney's skull had been fractured after a vicious beating.

David Dennis, a top CORE organizer, was asked by CORE leaders to give a eulogy at Chaney's funeral, but to maintain his cool. Dennis agreed, but at the pulpit—as the Chaney family grieved before him—his anger erupted.

> I've got vengeance in my heart tonight, and I ask you to feel angry with me. We've got to stand up. The best way we can remember James Chaney is to demand our rights. Don't just look at me and go back and tell folks you've been to a nice service. Your work is just beginning. . . . Stand up! Those neighbors who were too afraid to come to this service, pick them up and take them down there to register to vote! . . . Just tell them: 'Baby, I'm here!' Stand up! Hold your heads up! Don't bow down anymore! We want our freedom *now!*

While the Thirteenth Amendment had abolished slavery in 1865, whites in the Deep South kept their tight grip on black society for nearly a hundred years. Whites completely dominated government and law enforcement. They excluded blacks from good jobs, denied them proper education, and forced them to use inferior, segregated public facilities. African Americans who even attempted to register to vote risked being fired, harassed, beaten, or killed.

"Many say Mississippi is a bad place to live," stated a teenage Mississippian in 1964. "Well it is, if you hate going to the back of a street car, if you hate using the back door to a restaurant, and hate to hear a white call your parents girl and boy . . . . [I]f you hate all these things and many others, I join you in saying Mississippi is the worst state to live in."

In 1964, Bob Moses and SNCC, with the help of CORE, launched the Mississippi Summer Project. Their primary goals were to get black Mississippians registered to vote, establish "Freedom Schools" to give black children a proper education, and to organize the Mississippi Freedom Democratic Party to challenge the whites-only Mississippi Democratic Party. Helping them in their cause were hundreds of volunteers—mostly well-off white college students from northern universities.

The whites of Mississippi viewed SNCC, CORE, and the "outside agitators" from the North as hostile threats. In preparation for the influx of activities, law enforcement agencies added more officers and stockpiled firearms, while Ku Klux Klansmen chomped at the bit. "[T]his is going to be a long, hot summer," declared Charles J. Benner of the white supremacist States' Rights National Party, "but the 'heat' will be applied to the race-mixing TRASH by the DECENT people. . . . When your communist-oriented GOONS get to Mississippi, I hope they get their just dues."

As Freedom Summer approached, many black citizens worried that whites would violently vent their anger against African Americans. "Believe me, there were real reasons for folks to be afraid," wrote volunteer Chris Williams. "I worked in Batesville, and the echoes of the lynching of Emmett Till ten years earlier in next door Tallahatchie County were still in the air along with a thousand other incidents of violence against Afro-Americans."

Yet while some black citizens were afraid to leave their homes, others risked it all by venturing to the courthouse to register to vote. Volunteer Gloria Clark recalled that there "were adult men in their seventies who said to me, 'I want to register to vote before I die.'"

Like David Dennis, Fannie Lou Hamer was fed up and unwilling to accept anymore injustice. "We're tired of all this beatin',' we're tired of takin' this," she said. "It's been a hundred years and we're still being beaten and shot at, crosses are still being burned, because we want to vote. But I'm goin' to stay in Mississippi, and if they shoot me down, I'll be buried here."

In 1964, one year after Martin Luther King's "I Have a Dream" speech at the March on Washington, change was in the air. Wrote Williams: "In the summer of 1964 the number one song blasting out of the black juke joints . . . was Sam Cooke singing 'A Change Is Gonna Come. . . .' [T]he long suffering black citizenry suddenly saw a ray of hope after a long nightmare of oppression."

Throughout the churches of Mississippi during the middle months of 1964, Freedom Summer participants—black and white—locked arms and sang spirited freedom songs: "I'm on My Way," "Keep Your Eyes on the Prize," and "We Shall Overcome." It would indeed be a long, hot summer, but one that would profoundly change the state of Mississippi—and the nation.

two

Jim Crow's Stranglehold

N ew to Mississippi in 1964, Patti Miller wondered what was bulging in the cheeks of the poor African American children she came across. She assumed they could not have afforded candy, so it must have been something else.

"What are you eating?" she finally inquired.

"Dirt," they answered.

She couldn't believe what she heard. "What?" she asked.

"Dirt," they said.

"Can you show me?" she asked.

Several of the children pulled gray, claylike chunks of dirt out of their mouths. "The dirt had visible veins of minerals running through it," Miller wrote, "and the children in their bodies' wisdom, somehow knew that they could get needed minerals from the dirt."

In early '60s America, there was poverty and then there was black, Mississippi poverty. Few outside of the Magnolia State realized just how bad conditions were for Mississippi's African Americans. Growing up in the 1950s in a well-to-do area in Massachusetts, Gloria Clark was oblivious to the racial problems down south. "[W]hat you were taught about is that there was slavery," she said. "Once they got rid of slavery, everything was fine."

Meanwhile, Mississippi governor Paul Johnson did his best to deflect attention from the racial atrocities in his state. "I think the Negro is well off and that he knows he's well off," he said. "He has confidence in the . . . leadership of his state. He's like the Filipino. He just wants to be left alone."

Larry Taylor, an African American from Como, Mississippi, told a different story.

> Where I grew up in Mississippi in the '50s and '60s, life for black people was very difficult and sometimes very frightening. As children, we had to walk to school down the main street of our town. White men would call us names and make us walk around them as we walked . . . . The way we had to live, and where we had to live, was very depressing. At that time, black people didn't make enough money to feed their families, if they had two or more children. And because of that, they raised pigs and chickens right in the neighborhood. The smell of the animals along with the outdoor toilets were sometimes almost unbearable in the summertime.

In 1960, Mississippi was the poorest state in America—and black citizens in the state fared far worse than whites. The median salary of black Mississippians was $1,444, the lowest in the nation. Moreover, it was only a third of what Mississippi whites earned. The typical black person in

A group of poor African American children stand in front of their house in Palmers Crossing, Mississippi. (© *Herbert Randall, McCain Library & Archives, University of Southern Mississippi*)

Mississippi had only a sixth-grade education, and only about 7 percent finished high school.

Economically enslaved, many rural blacks stooped and picked cotton for three dollars a day. Large numbers lived in dilapidated, tar-paper shacks with no electricity. Almost half of the black citizens in Mississippi in 1960 lacked running water, while nearly two-thirds didn't have toilets. Farm workers were perpetually in debt to white landowners.

As in Alabama and other areas in the Jim Crow South, Mississippi remained segregated in the early 1960s. From schools and hospitals to public restrooms and drinking fountains, African Americans had to make do with separate and inferior facilities.

The whites in the state insisted that it was black people's own fault that they couldn't rise above poverty. Generations of whites perpetuated the myth that African Americans were dumb and lazy. Certainly, said Senator James Eastland (D-MS), "[N]o one wants to deny the Negro economic opportunity or economic equality." He added, "It is a historic fact that southern white people are the best friends he has ever had."

In reality, the state's laws and customs—created and enforced by whites—made it almost impossible for blacks to get ahead. Freedom Summer volunteer Deborah Rand recalled a black man who worked in Pascagoula, Mississippi. "He was a laborer—the lowest paid job at the shipyard," she wrote. "He told us that he was constantly training white men, but that the whites got promoted to higher paid jobs while he and all the other black workers remained as laborers."

Nor could black children "rise above" through education, because Mississippi's black schools were woeful. In the United States, all young citizens were (and are) entitled to free and adequate education from kindergarten through high school, but Mississippi's black schools were far from adequate. Even though the U.S. Supreme Court had demanded the abolishment of segregated school systems back in 1954, Mississippi (like many states) continued the practice.

More alarmingly, the state spent four times more money educating a white pupil ($81.86 in 1964) than a black student ($21.77). Counties also funded the schools, but they too short-shafted African American students; South Pike County contributed $59.95 annually for each white pupil and $1.35 for each black student. North Pike County chipped in $30.89 each for whites and $0.76 each for blacks.

According to author Len Holt, whites considered African American students "backward, dull, imbecilic, slothful." In

Black children in the South often had to attend overcrowded, dilapidated schools with limited resources. *(Library of Congress)*

reality, black students were placed in highly disadvantaged learning situations. The decrepit schools were cold and drafty in the winter. Children of multiple ages were mixed together, and teachers (who were grossly underpaid) lacked proper supplies.

"We had hand-me-down books for school that came from the white people," recalled Taylor. "Most of the time, they were old and outdated." He added that the exceptionally poor kids on plantations "barely had clothes to wear to school. And with no cafeteria in the school, they had no lunch most of the time."

Mississippi was one of two states in the early 1960s that did not require public education. Black youths on plantations started school weeks late because they were needed to

The inside of a school for black children *(Library of Congress)*

pick cotton. "I went to school for two years," a black woman named Amanda told author Sally Belfrage, "but they didn't have no books and we wasn't learnin' nothin', so my father took us out and made us chop cotton."

Perhaps worst of all, most whites treated African Americans as subservient, even subhuman. Blacks were expected to address white men as "sir," while whites called black men "boy." "Uppity" blacks risked being fired, arrested, or worse. In 1955, Emmett Till was lynched for flirting with a white woman. In fact, from 1882 to 1962, 538 African Americans in Mississippi were lynched—more than in any other state. Many were lynched for the pettiest of infractions, such as talking to a white woman.

Like slaves of a hundred years earlier, many African Americans constantly feared that whites would figuratively or literally "crack the whip." Robert Hargreaves, a white Freedom Summer volunteer from Michigan State, remembered frequenting a black establishment in Mississippi. "An old black man had his back turned to me and was moaning to himself about how hard the whites were on him," Hargreaves wrote. "Then he turned around and saw me and paled. He spent the whole rest of the evening . . . saying, 'Nosuh! Nosuh! I didn't mean nothing, suh!' Nothing I said would convince him that I was on his side! There was real fear in his pleadings."

In the United States, the democratic process theoretically allows voters to correct social injustice. Citizens in black communities can vote black candidates into office. They can elect city council members, mayors, judges, and state representatives. But in Mississippi up through the early 1960s, those in power—all of whom were white—denied African Americans the opportunity to vote, flagrantly violating federal law.

Because more than 45 percent of Mississippi's citizens were black, the state's whites knew that they would lose substantial power if they allowed African Americans to vote. In the counties in which the majority of citizens were black, whites had even more to fear. "Do not let a single nigger vote," Senator Eugene Bilbo (D-MS) warned in 1946. "If you let a few register and vote this year, next year there will be twice as many, and the first thing you know, the whole thing will be out of hand."

Whites created an elaborate system to prevent blacks from voting—or even registering to vote. Citizens could register to vote only on certain days; black applicants found that their line moved at a snail's pace. They could wait all day and not get to the front of the line. Mississippi law stated that citizens could register to vote only if they read and interpreted a section of the state constitution. Whether they interpreted it satisfactorily was up to the discretion of the white registrars. The overwhelming majority of African Americans, even those with doctoral degrees, failed such tests.

Meanwhile, registrars passed white voter-registration applicants no matter how bad their answers were. In George County, a white applicant had to interpret this section: "There shall be no imprisonment for debt." His answer: "I thank that a Neorger should have 2 years in collage before voting because he don't under stand." He passed.

Whites also used intimidation to prevent blacks from voting. Large numbers of African Americans were fired for trying to register. Local newspaper editors even listed these applicants' names in the paper, making them marked targets for employers. Moreover, it was not uncommon for Ku Klux Klansmen to intimidate or assault voting applicants.

As a result of all the exclusionary and intimidation practices, only 6.7 percent of blacks in Mississippi were registered to vote in 1960. This was by far the lowest figure of black registration in the United States. In 1962, five counties with a majority black population had zero black registrants. Black civil rights leaders knew that the only way to improve conditions in Mississippi was to bust up the white power structure—and the only way to do that was to help African Americans exercise their right to vote.

The civil rights movement had begun in earnest in 1955, but states besides Mississippi bore the fruit of the efforts. Neighboring Alabama had success in 1955 with the Montgomery bus boycott and in 1963 with

Klansmen drive through a black neighborhood with a noose on display in order to intimidate African Americans and keep them from voting. *(Library of Congress)*

desegregation in Birmingham. Mississippi remained a tough nut to crack.

While Martin Luther King and his Southern Christian Leadership Conference (SCLC) took the lead in Alabama, SNCC (called "Snick") headed civil rights activism in Mississippi. SNCC emerged in spring 1960 at Shaw University in Raleigh, North Carolina. Some of the SNCC pioneers found success that year with lunch counter sit-ins—sitting at all-white counters in department stores until they were served. Many such demonstrations, and the media attention accompanying them, finally pressured store chains to desegregate their lunch counters.

Like King, SNCC believed—morally and strategically—in nonviolent protest. In August 1960, SNCC worker Marion Barry (the future mayor of Washington, D.C.) began teaching nonviolent protest methods to black teenagers in Mississippi. Some of the teens staged sit-ins and were subsequently jailed. SNCC and CORE also employed nonviolent tactics in the 1961 Freedom Rides. Challenging the federal law that prohibited segregation on interstate bus travel, black and white Freedom Riders rode Greyhound and Trailways buses in the Deep South. Many were beaten in Alabama and arrested in Mississippi, but they shone a light on southern bigotry for the rest of the nation to see.

The SNCC worked relentlessly to register voters in Mississippi. White resistance, however, was ferocious. On September 25, 1961, Herbert Lee, a father of nine, tried to become the first black citizen from McComb County to register to vote as part of SNCC's efforts. In retaliation, he was shot and killed by E. H. Hurst, a local legislator. Hurst was subsequently acquitted by an all-white jury. Lewis Allen, an African American who witnessed the murder, was also killed.

The determined SNCC workers forged on, but the violence continued. "While in Walthall County, Tylertown, Mississippi," wrote John W. Hardy, "I was pistol whipped by the Election Registrar and later arrested by the Sheriff while attempting to register several local older black residents. I was released from jail a day after experiencing what seemed like an eternity. I was smuggled out of Mississippi under the cover of darkness."

In September 1962, the eyes of the nation focused on Oxford, Mississippi, as James Meredith attempted to become the first African American to enroll at the University of Mississippi. Though a federal district court ordered the school to admit Meredith, Mississippi governor Ross Barnett sent state police to bar his admission. Only after Barnett was found guilty of contempt of court was Meredith allowed to register. But when he did, white students and locals rioted in protest. Two men were killed, 160 sustained injuries, and President John F. Kennedy sent 23,000 U.S. troops to quell the violence.

That same year, the Council of Federated Organizations (COFO) was organized to coordinate voter registration in the South. SNCC members provided the great majority of the staff, but CORE, the NAACP, and the SCLC also contributed support. Again, Mississippi was the most dangerous battleground. On February 28, 1963, a white man shot into a car of black activists. They hit one man, Jimmy Travis, and just missed one of SNCC's top organizers, Bob Moses.

In spring 1963, NAACP Field Director Medgar Evers made the most brazen challenge yet to Jim Crow in Mississippi. He launched a campaign against segregation in Jackson, the state's largest city. Determined to stop it, Mayor Allen Thompson went on television, telling Jackson's black residents, "Do not listen to false rumors which will stir you, worry you, and upset you."

With the help of the Federal Communications Commission, Evers was able to make a televised response a week later. He

Medgar Evers

talked about "a city of over 150,000, of which forty percent is Negro, in which there is not a single Negro policeman or policewoman, school crossing guard, fireman, clerk, stenographer." Blacks in Mississippi, he said, wanted segregation abolished and they wanted the right to vote. Evers's passionate plea earned praise from the (relatively) progressive whites in Jackson. However, it also enraged the state's ardent segregationists. On June 12, Evers was assassinated on his front lawn by white supremacist Byron de la Beckwith.

Considering this avalanche of white backlash, SNCC's goal of mass voter registration seemed impossible. But hope was not lost. In July 1963, a white liberal from New York walked into the SNCC office in Jackson and offered an ingenious idea—one that would befuddle the segregationists. From that day forward, the momentum turned in Mississippi.

three
Northern Whites Join the Fight

Allard Lowenstein was the right man with the right idea in July 1963. Instead of officially registering African Americans to vote in Mississippi, he said, SNCC should register them for a mock gubernatorial election. The purpose would be twofold: to show America that black citizens in Mississippi wanted to vote (whites had blamed low voter registration figures on black apathy), and to give blacks confidence and experience in the voting process. SNCC leaders embraced the idea. It would be called the "Freedom Vote," and citizens would vote for "Freedom Party" candidates.

SNCC would have far greater success getting black citizens to participate in the Freedom Vote than having them go through the official voter-registration process. For one thing, Freedom Vote registrants wouldn't have to go to the courthouse (risking their jobs and their life) or pass nearly impossible tests. SNCC also saw added benefits: The process would strengthen SNCC/COFO's organizational abilities in the state, and the Freedom Vote would likely generate positive national media exposure.

After the state primary elections in August 1963, SNCC's Bob Moses spearheaded the Freedom Vote campaign. It would parallel the Democratic and Republican gubernatorial campaigns that would culminate in elections that November. To get the word out, Moses and Lowenstein recruited sixty white students from Yale and Stanford.

These volunteers went door-to-door in black neighborhoods, informing residents of the practice election. Aaron Henry, a black pharmacist and the chairman of COFO, would be the mock candidate for governor. Reverend Edwin King, a white chaplain at an all-black college, was Henry's running mate as lieutenant governor. Although some of the COFO workers and white volunteers were beaten and arrested, they successfully spread the word.

On "election" day, black residents turned out in droves at the neighborhood voting sites. They voted at tables set up on sidewalks and at black-owned businesses, such as barbershops. All told, more than 90,000 African Americans cast their ballots.

Moses and SNCC deemed the Freedom Vote, and the use of volunteers, a great success. But of course, it was only a trial run. Blacks needed to vote in real elections to create real, positive changes in government. In late 1963, Moses proposed an ambitious voter-registration plan for 1964. SNCC workers heartily supported him. However, one issue engendered considerable debate: whether northern white volunteers should be allowed to participate.

Some SNCC veterans were hostile to the idea of teaming up with whites. They had been oppressed by white people

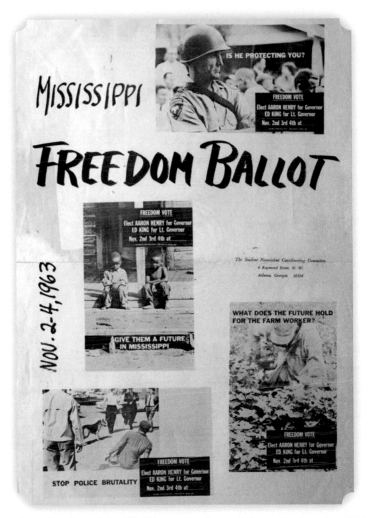

This flyer distributed by SNCC was used to publicize the Freedom Vote.
(Courtesy of Will D. Campbell Papers, McCain Library & Archives, University of Southern Mississippi)

all their lives, and their appeals to the white leadership in Washington had largely fallen on deaf ears. They wanted nothing to do with whites, period. Others argued that the highly educated, high-achieving whites would assume leadership roles within COFO. This would stunt the organization's plan to foster leadership skills among young black COFO members, and reinforce the caste system of dominant whites and submissive blacks.

Proponents of including white volunteers pointed out that SNCC's goal was integration, and thus it would be hypocritical to ban white members. "If we're going to break down this barrier of segregation," said SNCC member Fannie Lou Hamer, "we can't segregate ourselves." More practically, COFO would greatly benefit from the labor of hundreds of additional volunteers, regardless of skin color. As it was, SNCC membership was fairly small (in the dozens), as few black citizens were willing to face the severe risks that came with membership.

Moses believed that white volunteers would be necessary. His staff was too small to make much progress in registration, and it risked being obliterated altogether by white crackdowns. He would need as large an "army" as possible for his 1964 campaign. Just as importantly, SNCC leaders realized the public relations value of using volunteers of prominent white families. If they would come, the national media surely would follow. Moreover, their arrests and abuse likely would trigger outrage in the North, forcing intervention by the federal government. Summed up Moses: "[T]hese students bring the rest of the country with them. They're from good schools and their parents are influential. The interest of the country is awakened and when that happens, the government responds to that issue."

At a COFO meeting in December, participants proposed to limit the number of white volunteers to one hundred. Later, however, the SNCC Executive Committee discarded that proposal and decided to use as many people as necessary the following summer to help black Mississippians register to vote.

From there, the big question remained: Just how many white people would, for no pay, want to risk their lives for black people in Mississippi? Because of the spirit of the times, the answer was many.

Up through World War II, northern whites had been largely uninformed or apathetic about the plight of southern black citizens. Whites endured their own economic problems during the Great Depression of the 1930s, and war preoccupied their lives through 1945. But during the relative calm and unprecedented prosperity of the 1950s, whites outside the South started to examine racial injustice more closely. Whites of the era were also more educated, and the media addressed southern bigotry in greater detail. In 1955, the Montgomery bus boycott dominated headlines, as did the lynching of Emmett Till.

"Emmett Till was a fourteen-year-old who was brutally killed by a lynching mob in Mississippi in 1955," wrote Heather Tobis Booth, a white woman, "supposedly for looking the 'wrong way' at a white woman. I saw photos of his beaten body when I was a very young teenager and felt we cannot let something like this happen in our country."

As the civil rights movement picked up steam, northern whites became increasingly empathetic to the plight of southern blacks—largely because of the movement's emphasis on nonviolent protest. TV footage from Little Rock, Arkansas (1957), Albany, Georgia (1962), and Birmingham, Alabama (1963) showed southern whites, referred to sometimes as "crackers," reacting violently to law-abiding black protesters who simply wanted to go to school, register to vote, or order a sandwich at a white lunch counter.

"I have always felt that the people in the civil rights movement were the most courageous and inspiring Americans of my generation," wrote Deborah Rand, a Freedom Summer volunteer. "I was in awe of the sheer beauty of the people who sat down at lunch counters, picketed stores, participated in Freedom Rides, got arrested

Emmett Till *(Library of Congress)*

demanding the right to vote, and demanded that the United States become a real democracy."

Kay Michener explained why she signed up for Freedom Summer: "I saw a documentary on Channel 11 in Chicago about an integrated group who took a ferry ride near New Orleans and were all arrested," she wrote. "I was appalled. When I found out through SNCC that black people were systematically prevented from voting all through the South, I realized that democracy in the USA was not working and could not survive unless everyone was voting."

Gloria Clark said that the racism of Bull Connor, the public safety commissioner in Birmingham, inspired her to fight for civil rights. She was incensed by a TV interview of Connor, who was holding police dogs by his side as he talked to a reporter.

"I remember his response was, 'We don't need ya'll whites coming down,'" Clark said. "'We don't need ya'll Northerners to come down here. We can take care of our nigras ourselves.' I've never forgotten this line: 'We can take care of our nigras ourselves.' . . . I said, 'Am I living in the same country with this man?' . . . And I said no way is he going to define how people are treated in the country I live in. No way do I want a man like that defining it."

John F. Kennedy of Massachusetts, elected president in 1960, also was determined to end segregation. Young and charismatic, Kennedy declared in his inaugural address that he represented a "new generation of leadership." Many young whites were enamored with JFK's progressive views. They sat at attention when he addressed the nation on June 11, 1963:

> [A]re we to say to the world and much more importantly to each other, that this is a land of the free except for the Negroes; that we have no second-class citizens except Negroes; that we have no class or caste system, no ghettoes, no master race except with respect to Negroes? Now the time has come for this nation to fulfill its promise.

Certainly many white idealists were ready to follow JFK's lead and help the less fortunate. In 1960, 250 students—many inspired by Kennedy—formed Americans Committed to World Responsibility. Two years after JFK launched the Peace Corps in 1961, more than 7,000 American volunteers—

President John F. Kennedy

typically whites from well-to-do families—were serving on
the Corps' behalf in more than forty countries. When the
March on Washington was staged with Kennedy's blessing
on August 28, 1963, a large fraction of the 250,000 people in
attendance was white. That afternoon, Martin Luther King
inspired millions of Americans, white and black, with his "I
Have a Dream" speech.

In the fall of 1963, as Gallup Poll respondents proclaimed that civil rights was the most important crisis facing the nation, white Americans were eager to lock arms with their black brothers and sisters. Stated David Harris: "Freeing the Negroes of Mississippi seemed an admirable cause and fit easily into my search of 'great things' to do."

For some young activists, the assassination of Kennedy on November 22, 1963, made them more determined to fight for civil rights. As Freedom Summer volunteer Paul Cowan wrote, "The Mississippi Summer Project seemed the best place to commemorate him."

After sixty volunteers had ventured into Mississippi in 1963—and were lauded as heroes for their actions—hundreds more were ready to sign up for 1964's Freedom Summer. Booth said she "was quite frightened about going to Mississippi." But, she added, "I also realized that I would be facing some problems for a summer. The African Americans who lived there faced that their whole life. This country belonged to all of us, and we needed to make it work for everyone."

Added volunteer Bruce Hartford, "We used to say: 'If you don't like the history they're teaching you in school, go out and make some of your own.'"

And so they did.

four

Preparing for Battle

J anuary 1964 was a relatively quiet time in the United States, as Americans continued to mourn the death of President Kennedy. But things were changing. Turmoil was brewing in Vietnam, and the Beatles were preparing for their first visit to America in February. And down in the Deep South, COFO (Council of Federated Organizations) staff members approved a plan for the Mississippi Summer Project, also known as Freedom Summer.

Although the COFO staff approved of the basic plan for the project, they faced myriad problems, including the fact that the organization was pretty much broke. In addition, the SCLC (Southern Christian Leadership Conference) and the NAACP—though COFO members—were not eager to contribute to the Project. CORE agreed to fund 20 percent of the Summer Project, leaving SNCC to shoulder roughly 80 percent of the load. With no time to waste, COFO staffers got to work.

You Can Help Too

When a Student Nonviolent Coordinating Committee field secretary began work in Marshall County, Mississippi in the summer of 1962, he had to ride a mule from settlement to settlement.

When a SNCC vote project began in Wilcox County, Alabama, the SNCC worker there took to mule back also.

Neither worker was trying to impress the local citizens. They just didn't have cars.

Both of them do now, but Mississippi and Alabama roads are rough on mules and cars, and neither last very long.

You can help SNCC's registration and direct action programs in the South by supplying a field worker – or a project – with a car, bus or truck.

For further information, write:

CARS FOR FREEDOM
Student Nonviolent Coordinating Committee
6 Raymond Street
Atlanta 14, Georgia

This SNCC flyer was distributed as part of a fundraising effort for the Freedom Summer project. *(Courtesy of Will D. Campbell Papers, McCain Library & Archives, University of Southern Mississippi)*

In March, members sent literature and project applications to Friends of SNCC chapters and other civil rights groups at more than two hundred colleges and universities. SNCC especially focused on Ivy League schools and other elite universities. Interested applicants were told of the goals of the Mississippi project:

❏ register African-American voters throughout the state
❏ establish Freedom Schools for black children
❏ establish community centers, at which black citizens could get medical and legal assistance
❏ form the legally constituted Mississippi Freedom Democratic Party as a challenge to the all-white Mississippi Democratic Party

Volunteers were told they would not be paid; in fact, they would be asked to bring hundreds of dollars with them for personal necessities, food, and potential bail money. Despite the many drawbacks, hundreds of aspiring volunteers completed applications and returned them to SNCC headquarters in Jackson.

Of the 736 people who applied, 123 were students at Harvard, Yale, Princeton, and Stanford—arguably the most prestigious universities in America. Most of the remaining applicants attended other highly respected universities, such as Berkeley and Michigan. These students were socially conscious, confident in their abilities to improve America, and affluent enough to afford the trip and expenses.

While Freedom Summer organizers did not try to dissuade African Americans from applying, less than 10 percent of applicants were black. The main reason for this was that less than 3 percent of America's college students were

African American. A little more than 40 percent of applicants were women.

Most of those who applied were juniors, seniors, graduate students, or recent graduates. Many were already affiliated with civil rights groups, including CORE and SNCC, and the vast majority had some activist experience. Many of the applicants were aspiring teachers who were eager to apply their skills in Freedom Schools. Others were motivated by religious reasons. As one applicant stated, "Christ called us to *act* in the service of brotherhood, not just talk about it. I'm tired of talking. Mississippi is my opportunity to act."

Not all of those who applied actually made it to Freedom Summer. Those under twenty-one were required to get their parents' permission, and many parents refused to give it. "My parents, who were so loving and such good people, were so frightened that they did not want me to go," one volunteer, Heather Tobis Booth, wrote. "My mother could not talk, but only cry. My father feared for my life." Other applicants, after hearing news stories about the impending violent summer in Mississippi, backed out on their own.

In addition to those who voluntarily backed out, some applicants were rejected by SNCC interviewers. COFO leaders did not want mavericks or hotshots on the project; they wanted people who would work within the system. In addition, COFO rejected some women who were especially attractive or who gave indications that they would be open to sexual relations with a black man. Though this seemed to be sexist, COFO leaders knew how volatile southern white men could get about sex between a black male and a white woman. Such a scenario in Rosewood, Florida, in 1923, incited whites to burn and raze the whole town.

SNCC staff members conduct an orientation session for Freedom Summer volunteers in Oxford, Ohio. (© *Herbert Randall, McCain Library & Archives, University of Southern Mississippi*)

Those volunteers who remained attended orientation at Western College for Women in Oxford, Ohio, in June. The National Council of Churches sponsored two sessions, each a week long. The first one, from June 14 to 20, was for those who would work in voter registration. The following week's session was for Freedom School teachers.

COFO leaders pulled no punches with the recruits. For one thing, they let everyone know who was in charge. Moses may have been a bespectacled, Harvard-trained educator, but he came across as a forceful leader. Volunteer Chris Williams recalled: "Bob Moses made it very clear during orientation in Oxford, Ohio, that our role was as facilitators and organizers in support of the indigenous leadership; we were passing through but this was their state and their movement, and the struggle would be played out long after we were gone."

Moses told the recruits:

> Don't come to Mississippi this summer to save the Mississippi Negro. Only come if you understand, really understand, that his freedom and yours are one. . . . Maybe we're not going to get very many people registered this summer. Maybe, even, we're not going to get very many people into Freedom Schools. Maybe all we're going to do is live through this summer. In Mississippi, that will be so much!

Many of the instructors, such as firebrand leader Stokely Carmichael, wore the unofficial SNCC "uniform": blue denim overalls. They captivated the volunteers with stories of the violence that had occurred in Mississippi and likely would occur that summer. In a speech on June 18, black attorney R. Jess Brown told the volunteers of the upcoming danger. "Although you may be as white as a sheet, you will become as black as tar," he said. "You're going to be classified into two groups in Mississippi: niggers and nigger-lovers. And they're tougher on nigger-lovers."

SNCC's James Forman told volunteers that they all could expect to be arrested, jailed, beaten, and in many cases shot at. "I may be killed," he said. "You may be killed. The whole staff may go." He told volunteers to go quietly to jail if they were arrested, because "Mississippi is not the place to start conducting constitutional law classes for the policemen, many of whom don't have a fifth-grade education."

Immediately, the orientation speakers had a powerful effect on the volunteers. Said Frank Cieciorka, "I was mostly impressed with how smart and articulate the SNCC staff was." William Hodes wrote in a letter, "They tend to be suspicious of us, because we are white, Northern, urban, rich, inexperienced. We are somewhat in awe of them, and conscious of our own inferiority."

At the same time, volunteers sensed the profound significance of this undertaking. Reporters, including those from national magazines and the television networks, roamed the campus. Even John Doar, deputy chief of the U.S. Department of Justice's Civil Rights Division, came and talked to the volunteers. "There is no federal police force," Doar warned them. "The responsibility for protection is that of the local police." Many of the volunteers booed that comment, surprising Doar with their brazen response.

In addition to the many speeches, volunteers learned their duties for the summer and practiced them in workshops. Would-be teachers studied a booklet written by Charlie Cobb, a former Howard University student who came up with the idea for the Freedom Schools. Teachers would emphasize not just the "three Rs" (reading, writing, and arithmetic) but also leadership development and nonacademic curriculum. SNCC veterans even showed the recruits what to do if physically assaulted:

SNCC Field Secretaries Bruce Gordon (left) and Cordell Hull Reagon demonstrate nonviolent self-defense techniques. (© Herbert Randall, McCain Library & Archives, University of Southern Mississippi)

curl up and cover their heads to avoid damage to the face and vital organs.

Meanwhile, Mississippi law enforcement officials geared up for what they were calling an "invasion." A *Columbus Commercial Dispatch* headline declared: "Mississippians Not Going to Be Run Over." Warned a *Neshoba Democrat* editorial in April: "Outsiders who come in here and try to stir up trouble should be dealt with in a manner they won't forget."

By June, state legislators had even passed new laws in preparation for Freedom Summer. They outlawed the distribution of leaflets that called for public boycotts, and they banned picketing of public buildings.

While the black sections of Jackson were in desperate need of public funding, the city instead poured its money into the police force. The department purchased two hundred new shotguns and beefed up its police force from 390 members to 450. Each man was issued a gas mask in case tear gas was used to disperse demonstrators. Mayor Allen Thompson could also count on deputies, state troopers, and neighborhood citizen patrols.

The police department's motor fleet included "Thompson's Tank" and three enormous trailer trucks, which would cart demonstrators to two large detention compounds. "They are not bluffing, and we are not bluffing," Mayor Thompson said. "We're going to be ready for them. . . . They won't have a chance."

As it turned out, "trouble" started immediately, on the first day of summer. The first round of volunteers had just finished their orientation, and those in the second group were just beginning theirs. It was then, on June 21, that three volunteers—Michael Schwerner, James Chaney, and Andrew

This photo from an SNCC brochure shows the police force in Jackson, Mississippi, augmented in preparation for the arrival of Freedom Summer volunteers. *(Courtesy of Zoya Zeman Papers, McCain Library & Archives, University of Southern Mississippi)*

Goodman—were murdered in Mississippi. Up in Oxford, Ohio, volunteers were numbed by the news.

Rita Schwerner, wife of murdered activist Michael, began working with SNCC in Mississippi well before Freedom Summer got underway. After Michael disappeared, she spoke at an orientation session. Volunteer Robert Hargreaves remembered the moment:

> She got on stage and announced that her husband and two others had gone to investigate a church burning the day before and never returned. She described the security precautions to be used for the summer—always sign in and out with the time, destination, and expected time of return; never travel alone; never travel at night, etc. She then told of the frantic calls to hospitals, police, sheriffs. She broke down in tears—she had concluded they were already dead!

Many of the volunteers were scared, but few dropped out of the project. If anything, the troubling news about the three missing men made them even more determined to carry out their mission. On June 25 in Oxford, about a hundred volunteers watched a story about the disappearance on *CBS News*. Anchorman Walter Cronkite stated that the whole country was watching Mississippi. CBS played the civil rights anthem "We Shall Overcome," and the volunteers—joining hands—sang along.

"We're moving the world," an African American said after they finished singing. "We're all here to bring all the people of Mississippi, all the peoples of this country, all the peoples of the world . . . together . . . we're bringing a new revolution of love, so let's sing out together once again now, everybody hand in hand."

"Stunned, I walked alone out into the night," volunteer Stuart Rawlings wrote in his journal. "Life was beautiful. . . . These people were me, and I was them. Absolutely nothing came between us, as our hearts felt the call to work toward a better world."

Volunteers such as Rawlings felt they belonged to what was called a "beloved community." Others talked about experiencing a "freedom high." Emotions surged as the volunteers boarded busses that would transport them from Ohio to Mississippi. Blacks and whites locked arms and sang, and many tears were shed. "Kids were hanging out the windows kissing and hugging friends from the moving bus," recalled volunteer Ellen Lake. "It was a strange conglomeration of children headed for summer camp and children going off to war."

Soon, though, reality set in. "As the bus pulled out, a wave of terror hit me," wrote Patti Miller, who was on the bus.

> I was no longer on my safe college campus in Iowa. I was
> no longer headed for an orientation with others like myself in
> a different, but comfortable college setting. No, I was alone in
> a way I had never been. It seemed I was headed straight for an
> unknown no man's land. . . . The possibility that I too could
> die this summer became very real. I felt numb and a bit sick
> to my stomach.

"Bob Moses was on the bus I was on," remembered volunteer Kay Michener. "He sat there in his bib overalls and said quietly, 'I am going to Natchez [Mississippi]. Nobody has been working there and the Klan has said they will kill anybody who tries. I will go. I expect that I will be killed. I would not ask anybody to go with me. Anyone who goes with me will be killed as well.'"

For awhile no one spoke, but then "quiet voices broke the silence," recalled Michener. "'I will take the same chance as you.' 'I want to go with you.' 'I'll go too.'"

As the bus plunged toward the Deep South, Patti Miller overcame her fears: "Suddenly, I felt a wave of peace roll over me. I relaxed and felt more 'at home' than I ever had before. I might die. This was still true. But if I did, I knew it would be for a great purpose."

five

Welcome to Mississippi

O n June 20 and 21, 1964, 250 voter-registration volunteers arrived by bus in the Magnolia State. The next week, three hundred Freedom School and community center workers arrived. "When we saw that big sign that said, 'Welcome to Mississippi,' we felt like we had just crossed into enemy territory," remembered Jane Adams of Southern Illinois University. "Mississippi had geared up for war. They saw us as invaders coming in for a complete assault on their way of life. Everybody on both sides expected that there would be a bloodbath. We all expected we could die."

Michigan State student Robert Hargreaves sensed that threat immediately. "The Greyhound bus dropped us off on a residential street in Ruleville. We had no idea where we were. Almost immediately we found ourselves being circled by pickup trucks with rifles and big dogs in the back, driving very slowly around and around."

Black women whom Hargreaves had met at orientation picked up the stranded volunteers and drove off. Still, they would not feel safe for the remainder of the summer. Mississippi was a whole world away from the comfortable communities from which most of the volunteers hailed. Karen Jo Koonan of UCLA (University of California at Los Angeles) was among the many who were immediately overwhelmed. "The day I arrived," she wrote, "two babies had died of starvation." Volunteer Jonathan Steele recalled:

> My first Mississippi visit was a shock. We took part in crowded church-hall rallies that were invaded by heavy-set fire marshals, who ordered everyone out because the meetings allegedly constituted a fire hazard. In a modern church in Biloxi, we had to cower behind pillars in the aisle when local white thugs threw volleys of stones through the plate-glass windows. We were tailed by state troopers who pulled our cars over for minor infractions, or slapped on fines for obstruction because the car was parked more than two inches from the curb. Several of us were arrested. A few were beaten.

Joseph Keesecker remembered his "welcoming" to Mississippi:

> They took us to the police station, took our pictures, with signboards hanging from our necks, with our names on them. [They] gave us a stern lecture, laced with profanities, about why we shouldn't be there, how we had better be very careful because they couldn't and wouldn't protect us from the locals who were "justifiably" angry at us outsiders.

As the volunteers arrived at the various COFO offices, all the talk was about the disappearances of three fellow Freedom Summer recruits: Michael Schwerner, Andrew

SCHWERNER   CHANEY   GOODMAN

The FBI distributed these pictures of Michael Schwerner, James Chaney, and Andrew Goodman after they disappeared while working near Philadelphia, Mississippi. *(Courtesy of AP Images)*

Goodman, and James Chaney. On June 21, the three had driven to the site of a burned church outside Philadelphia in east-central Mississippi. The trio went to investigate the arson and express their sympathies to the congregation. Since Schwerner and Goodman were white and Chaney black, they were a prime target for police. Around 3 p.m., Neshoba County Deputy Sheriff Cecil Price pulled over their car. The young men were jailed briefly and then released, but after that they disappeared.

When the three failed to check in with Freedom Summer headquarters, staffers called the police. A day later the FBI became involved, and the incident erupted into a huge national story. As Bob Moses and SNCC had predicted, the skin color of the victims was a key factor in attracting national attention. America's northern white population could empathize with the likeable Schwerner, twenty-four, a hardworking, idealistic, Cornell University graduate who had named his cocker spaniel Gandhi. Goodman, age twenty, hailed from the Upper West Side of Manhattan. His parents had connections, including famed attorney Martin Popper, who became the family spokesperson in this case.

If only Chaney had disappeared, the story would have attracted only a fraction of the media attention and probably no federal intervention. As it was, President Lyndon Johnson sent two hundred sailors to the area to help the FBI search the swamps and countryside for the missing men. Chillingly, they uncovered the bodies of two black men who had been lynched, Charles Moore and Henry Dee.

As the search dragged on, some whites in Mississippi blamed the victims. Said Neshoba County Sheriff Lawrence Rainey, "If they're missing, they're just hid somewhere trying to get a lot of publicity out of it, I figure." Former Mississippi governor Ross Barnett, who had strongly resisted the integration of the University of Mississippi two years earlier, had little sympathy for the victims. "Of course I don't approve of murder," Barnett stated, "but those kids were asking for trouble."

Keesecker and a fellow volunteer tried to understand how local whites felt about the story:

> We posed as college boys on a vacation trip. What we heard was a lot of talk about how [FBI chief J. Edgar] Hoover . . . and all those northern "trouble makers and outside agitators" had set up the fake disappearance of the three workers near Philadelphia. . . . This was coupled with assurance that "our niggahs" are really quite content here and the only thing stirring them up are the outsiders and "Martin Luther Coon."

On August 4, Americans discovered that the disappearance was anything but fake. The three bodies were discovered in an earthen dam on a farm outside Philadelphia, Mississippi. Each of the men had been shot, and Chaney's skull had been fractured in a vicious beating. "In my twenty-five years as a pathologist and medical examiner," stated Dr. David Spain, who examined Chaney's body, "I have never seen bones so severely shattered." It would be months before any suspects were charged.

A day after the discovery, CORE representative Mimi Hernandez issued a statement. "We won't be intimidated," she declared. "As a matter of fact, the death of three workers will incite us to increase our forces in Mississippi."

As SNCC leaders had imagined, the martyrdom of white volunteers galvanized the North to fight against injustice in the Deep South. In newspapers across the country, readers were emotionally moved by a photo of the three mothers—Fannie Lee Chaney, Carolyn Goodman, and Anne Schwerner—linking arms as they left the church following the funeral service for Andrew Goodman.

Andrew's father, Robert Goodman, issued a statement that was published nationwide: "Our grief, though personal, belongs to the nation. The values our son expressed in his simple action of going to Mississippi are still the bonds that bind this nation together."

From the beginning of the summer, Freedom Project staffers worked day and night in their campaign for justice. The COFO leaders were exceptionally well organized. SNCC took control of four of Mississippi's five congressional districts, while CORE was in charge of the fifth. COFO staffed thirty-two projects throughout the state, from Holly Springs near Mississippi's northern border to Biloxi on the Gulf. Twelve more projects would be added later in the summer, as more

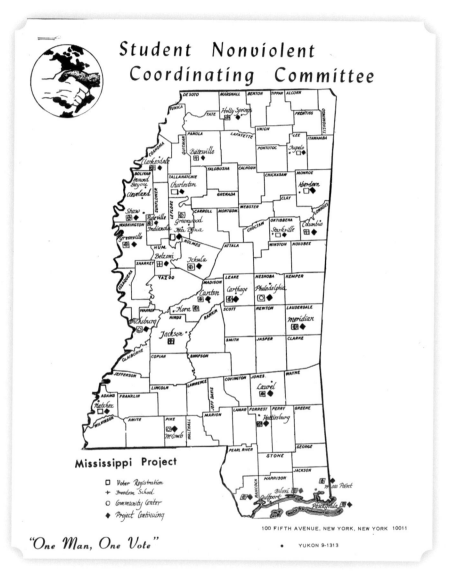

This map produced by the SNCC shows the Freedom Summer project locations in Mississippi. *(Courtesy of Matthew Zwerling Papers, McCain Library & Archives, University of Southern Mississippi)*

volunteers joined the Summer Project and leaders became even more ambitious.

Philadelphia, site of the triple murder, was located in District 4, but District 3—the southwest corner of the state—was considered the most perilous area. SNCC did not ignore this danger zone. The most hazardous District 3 projects were in Natchez, where Moses had predicted he would be killed, and McComb, where more than two-thirds of all bomb attacks would occur during the summer. Ku Klux Klan membership was exceptionally high in these two communities.

Each project was staffed by several to several dozen people. Most were voter-registration workers or Freedom School teachers, while others ran community centers or did office work. As they arrived in their various project areas, volunteers were struck by the dismal living conditions of black residents. "You could always tell the black part of town even when no people were present," remembered Robert Hargreaves, "because that's where the pavement, sidewalks, and streetlights ended. Most black homes were without gas or electricity."

Keesecker found many people "living in extreme poverty. I saw untreated health problems due to lack of funds, lack of education, and in some cases apparent (understandable) resignation in the face of what seemed insurmountable odds."

Chris Williams of Vermont was shocked by what he saw in Mississippi. "[J]obs above a menial level weren't available to blacks," he wrote, "and the income gap between black and white was so extreme that you could tell by just looking at a house if it was owned by blacks or whites. This was the land of American Apartheid."

In addition to the "No Coloreds" signs that prolifer-
ated in the state, recruits witnessed other evidence of Jim
Crow oppression—not just in rural areas but in cities too.
Kay Michener recalled a visit to Canton, Mississippi. "[A]s
we walked through downtown, we saw stickers on all the
businesses announcing membership in the White Citizens'
Council," she wrote. "National businesses such as Sears also
had the stickers."

For Mississippi's whites, generations of intimidation had
been effective. "[M]ost Mississippi blacks I met were diffi-
dent and afraid," stated Hargreaves. "Even when they knew
you were a volunteer, they had it beat into them to keep their
eyes downcast, shuffle their feet, and say 'Yassuh! Yassuh!'
in the presence of whites."

Chris Williams lived in a wood-frame house on the edge
of town with a black farming couple, Robert and Mona Miles,
and their two young children. "There were loaded guns behind
every door in the house," he recalled. "The whole side of
the house facing the road was riddled with bullets fired by
nightriders. When Robert's sister came down from Detroit to
visit, she said, 'Robert, why don't you fix your house. This
looks pitiful!' Robert replied, 'I just want everyone to know
just how mean these Mississippi white folks are.'"

Despite their fears, many African American families
welcomed the visitors from the North. They appreciated
the recruits' courage and commitment, as well as the
respect they showed the black citizens. For the first time
in their lives, whites referred to these individuals as "Mr."
and "Mrs." A large percentage of the volunteers lived with
local black families during the summer. "They opened
their homes, shared their food—literally gave their bed

Many African Americans welcomed the volunteers' presence in Mississippi. In this photo, local residents socialize with Freedom Summer volunteers at a community fish fry. (© *Herbert Randall, McCain Library & Archives, University of Southern Mississippi*)

over to us," wrote Heather Tobis Booth, who stayed with the Hawkins family.

Other African Americans were welcoming in other ways, such as making lunches for project workers, inviting volunteers over for Sunday dinner, or asking them to speak at church services. After a while, many of the African Americans who housed the recruits felt protective of them. Gloria Clark recalled that the bolder black citizens owned shotguns and were willing to use them to protect themselves, their families, and the white guests in their homes.

"They were the greatest," praised Clark. "They were ready for us. Some asked what took us so long to get there. They were extremely brave and ready to risk it all for the right to vote and exercise their civil and political rights."

"Every day I was there, I felt alive and energized,"

wrote volunteer Mark Weiss, who worked for six months in Clarksdale, Mississippi. "I felt accepted in a way I had never experienced before. Walking down the street, older black people would spontaneously come and take my hand in theirs and say how much they appreciated what we were doing. They clearly understood the risks we were taking."

By living with African American families, volunteers learned firsthand what poverty was all about. In lieu of expensive wallpaper, residents used newspaper. One volunteer recalled sharing a bed with a fellow project worker and three black children. In the rural communities, homes often lacked electricity, plumbing, and hot water. Those without plumbing relied on well water. Instead of toilets, they used outhouses, which reeked in the summer heat. With temperatures in the eighties and nineties and humidity high, volunteers could have used two showers a day. Instead, many bathed in wash tubs out back.

Not all of the volunteers were guests of families. Many lived in "Freedom Houses," which were often overcrowded,

Volunteer Virginia "Jinny" Glass washes her face in a tub. Many houses in the poverty-stricken black neighborhoods of Mississippi lacked indoor plumbing. (© *Herbert Randall, McCain Library & Archives, University of Southern Mississippi*)

messy, and unsanitary. "[Y]ou had to stomp your feet as you approached the bathroom in the Freedom House, so the rats would disappear," recalled Clark. "They would come up through the toilet!" Housing was such a problem that some workers slept in the project offices.

Volunteer Than Porter of Maryland explained the dangers involved with living with an African American family. "One time," Porter wrote, "a deputy sheriff came to the house with two pistols on his hips and said . . . 'Ah jis' come ou' cheah [out here] to see how y'all niggah lovers is gittin' along.'" Porter recalled that they had to bomb-proof their home. "[W]e blocked the space under the house to prevent anyone from throwing a Molotov cocktail under it," he wrote, "and we made a rule never to walk past a window even in the daytime. Somebody could shoot at a silhouette."

Based on their experiences in Mississippi, COFO created a *Summer Project Security Handbook* to keep volunteers safe. The book advised workers to study the county map and be aware of safe houses and sanctuaries in the county. It stated that they should keep interior car lights off at night and to be suspicious of cars that circled offices or Freedom Houses. It even warned against sleeping near an open window. Although probably few whites were willing to kill African Americans or the "outside agitators," many were ready to harass and even terrorize them. "It is the fear and uncertainty that is maddening," wrote a Greenwood volunteer. "I must always be on guard."

Kay Michener explained the pervasiveness of the harassment:

> All summer we avoided going out at night. . . . We stretched chicken wire over the Freedom House windows so that the bombs

Volunteers and residents join hands and sing "We Shall Overcome" during a mass meeting at True Light Baptist Church. (© *Herbert Randall, McCain Library & Archives, University of Southern Mississippi*)

would bounce off—and they did. Many of the cars were equipped with two-way radios, and a common practice of the Klan or White Citizens' Council was to radio a distress call supposedly from a civil rights worker and set up an ambush. Pickups with full gun racks in the cabs drove by constantly, the drivers leering and making obscene gestures. My brother, Charles Prickett, was a worker in Madison County, and he said that tacks usually got dumped on the roads while mass meetings were in progress. We were instructed not to sleep in the front of the house and not to sit on the porch. We were living in a war.

After volunteering in Mississippi, Hargreaves went to Vietnam when the war started to heat up. "But after Mississippi," he wrote, "living in a war zone was a vacation."

As the days and weeks wore on, some of the volunteers succumbed to the pressure and abandoned the project. Most stayed, however, and they were joined by several hundred new recruits. Many of these new volunteers had been inspired by the press accounts of Freedom Summer. In addition, a larger number of lawyers and doctors traveled to Mississippi to donate their services.

Periodically, project members and local black citizens gathered for mass meetings. In these gatherings, speakers inspired activists with their passionate pleas. All the while, participants bonded while singing Freedom Songs. "The songs of the movement often gave us strength," declared Heather Tobis Booth. "We sang 'We are not afraid' even when we were afraid."

"The Mass Meetings were our fuel," wrote Patti Miller. "One could enter a meeting feeling drained and alone and leave feeling energized and at one with every other person in the room or church. . . . It wasn't just the community of civil rights workers that was so electrifying, it was the black community that had so generously allowed us to join them—to be a part of and experience their magic."

six

Daring to Register

Joseph Keesecker knew that registering black citizens during the Summer Project would not be easy. However, he never dreamed how challenging it would be. One day, he and his partner crossed a stream to visit the occupants of an isolated shack in the woods.

We approached, knocked on the door, and were greeted by a man and a woman, probably in their sixties. We told them we were working for the Mississippi Freedom Democratic Party, and they showed no recognition for what that might be. Then we said we were doing civil rights work; still no recognition. Voter registration . . . blank. We talked about Martin Luther King, hoping that would make a connection, and the man said he had never heard of him. We mentioned JFK and got the same response.

I was dumbfounded by the realization that these people were living cut off from society, from news, from knowledge of and involvement in what was happening in their world with great importance for them. And we became aware that they were

SNCC Field Secretary Sandy Leigh (right) and local black activist Doug Smith (left) explain voter registration procedures to an elderly African American resident on his front porch. (© *Herbert Randall, McCain Library & Archives, University of Southern Mississippi*)

really afraid. We apologized for disturbing them and quickly left, hoping none of the whites had seen us around their place, very aware that we might have put them at risk for something about which they did not have a clue.

Of course, the range of political awareness varied greatly among Mississippi's black citizenry. College-educated black activists knew more about the political system than many of their Ivy League guests. For other African Americans in the state, all they knew about registering to vote was that it was strictly taboo.

Of the hundreds of volunteers, many were involved in voter-registration work. Their job was to canvas black neighborhoods, in both cities and rural areas, and convince citizens to register. Because of the dangers involved, COFO decided to use mostly male volunteers in this capacity. "I work in voter registration," wrote Robert Feinglass to his father. "On a normal day we roll out of bed early in the morning. . . . We study the map of a county, decide where we will work for the day. We scramble for breakfast and hit the road."

Feinglass drove almost two hundred miles a day, going from house-to-house. He and other registration workers were typically greeted the same way: when they pulled up in their cars, children would become frightened, often hiding behind their parents.

The volunteers could not believe the wretched living conditions of some of the residents. One worker was alarmed to find a baby lying on a cot on a porch. Flies covered the child's eyes, nose, and mouth. "The whole house," reported the worker, "seemed diseased, rotten, and splitting at the seams with infection."

Upon arriving at each house, volunteers would shake the adults' hands; for some, it was the first white person's hand they had ever held. The residents, especially in the early weeks of the Project, were typically suspicious. Many did not want to even talk about registration.

"The [black] professionals and land owners by and large welcomed us and were enthusiastic about our work," wrote Frank Cieciorka. "Sharecroppers were the hardest to reach because if the whites who owned the land they worked on found out they talked to us (let alone attempt to register to vote), they would quite possibly get kicked off the land and

Some African American residents were reluctant to talk to Freedom Summer volunteers for fear of being terrorized by local whites. (© Herbert Randall, McCain Library & Archives, University of Southern Mississippi)

have no means of livelihood. Often when I talked to share-croppers, I noticed they seemed apprehensive and would glance about to try to determine if any whites were around who might cause them trouble."

Hargreaves said most of the black citizens he visited would not even answer the door. "Once in a while," he wrote, "I would hear a voice coming from behind the door: 'Go away! I don't want to get killed!' Once, a disembodied voice went on to say, 'You see that woman on the porch at the end of the street?' 'Yes.' 'Well, she tells the white folks everything she sees here.'"

Very few of the volunteers blamed the African Americans for being apprehensive. Instead, they became increasingly

angry with the white oppressors—local citizens, law enforcement, state legislators, and the federal government which had
allowed Jim Crow to flourish for a hundred years. "This is
really the most frightening thing about the whole situation,"
wrote Project worker William Hodes, "to see these masses
of people, including many no older than myself, with their
spirits crushed, just not seeming to care about anything."

Remarkably, many citizens did overcome their fears and
apathy and opened their doors to the volunteers. Once inside
the homes, however, the workers had to deliver a rather
complicated "sales pitch." First, they had to convince the
residents to officially register to vote. This meant that they
would have to go to the courthouse on the few days that it
was open for registration.

SNCC leaders, however, felt that regular registration
wasn't effective enough. They knew that only a small number of citizens would be registered that summer, and that the
Democratic Party—the dominant party in Mississippi—would
remain all white. Thus, on April 26, 1964, SNCC formed
its own legally constituted party, the Mississippi Freedom
Democratic Party (MFDP). They selected four U.S. congressional candidates: Fannie Lou Hamer, Victoria Gray, John
Houson, and Rev. John Cameron. In addition to trying to
get residents to register at the courthouse, volunteers asked
them to join the MFDP. They could do so immediately by
filling out a "Freedom Form."

Workers had much more luck convincing citizens to sign
the MFDP form, which whites didn't take seriously. However,
many black citizens strongly resisted going to the courthouse
to register. For many, the mere mention of "courthouse"
caused them to shudder. "The county seat for Leflore County

Victoria Gray's campaign headquarters during her run for the U.S. Senate on the Mississippi Freedom Democratic Party ticket (© *Herbert Randall, McCain Library & Archives, University of Southern Mississippi*)

is Greenwood," stated a letter from that city that was published in *Letters from Mississippi.* "This in itself restrains Negroes from voting because they don't like to go to the courthouse, which has bad connotations for them. Behind the courthouse is the Yazoo River. The river also has bad connotations; as Albert Darner said, it's 'Dat river where dey floats them bodies in.'"

Yet thanks to the success of the Freedom Vote the year before, black citizens became more willing to go to the courthouse to vote. As Freedom Summer progressed, their confidence and determination increased. Would-be registrants no longer felt vulnerable and on their own; they found strength and assurance in being part of a mass movement.

As SNCC staffer Ivanhoe Donaldson confirmed, "There was less fear in the Negro community about taking part in civil rights."

To intimidate African Americans, many local newspapers printed the names of those who registered to vote. This made them easy targets for employers or others who wanted to retaliate against them. Yet to black readers, this list of names was like an honor roll. They viewed those on the list as heroes, and many dreamed of the day that their names would be on the newspaper list.

Throughout Freedom Summer, a full 17,000 African Americans risked their livelihoods and their lives and went to the courthouse. Typically they wore their finest clothes. Not only did they want to look respectable and dignified, but for many this was the most monumental day of their lives. Volunteers were amazed by their courage. "I could not help but wonder," mused Cieciorka, a San Jose State student, "how many citizens of San Jose would be willing to risk their jobs, their homes, even their lives for the right to register to vote when they know they probably would fail the registration test."

Once at the courthouse, applicants inevitably faced delays, red tape, and other means of obstruction, and many were harassed. If they were patient and lucky enough, applicants got to take a test to prove that they were "qualified" to be a registered voter.

The difficulty of the tests depended on the whim of the government officials who created them. "[I]n 1964, county officials were known to administer the written test for registering to vote in Chinese," stated Kay Michener. "One wag, when presented with this test and asked if he could read the

Chinese version, replied, 'Sure I can read it. It says, 'Ain't no niggers gonna redish [register] today.'"

Of the 17,000 registration applicants in Mississippi in the summer of 1964, less than 1,700 were accepted and added to voter-registration rolls. Nine hundred of those were in Panola County, where, because of a successful lawsuit prior to the summer, federal officials oversaw voting procedures.

In the big picture, 1,700 new voters was not very significant. This accounted for less than one-thousandth of the state's population—hardly enough to make a dent in the white-dominated political structure. However, as the summer progressed, Project workers placed more faith in the MFDP campaign. So too did the state's black citizens. "Fear reigned at first," reported a Vicksburg volunteer, "but soon people were excited about the prospects of the party and neighbors were talking to neighbors about the 'New Thing.'"

Their anticipation would peak in August, when MFDP delegates would travel to New Jersey and participate in the Democratic National Convention. In the meantime, another group of Summer Project volunteers had a much different, though no less important, agenda. They operated the Summer Project's most famous legacy: the Freedom Schools.

seven

Freedom Schools

Theoretically, each of the thirty or so Freedom Schools were supposed to stress such basics as reading and math while addressing contemporary issues and developing leadership skills. As it turned out, though, each Freedom School took on a life of its own.

Wilfred Stone was among several volunteers who ran a Freedom School in "Dooderville," a black ghetto in Jackson. "I was the English teacher in the group and faced a 'class' of some thirty kids ranging in age from kindergarten to high school and in literacy from zero to (on a scale of 10) at least 9," Stone wrote. "So we created a curriculum, swapped stories, made up plays, acted them out, started a newspaper. I also took kids to lunch around the corner [as some garage mechanics glowered at us from across the street, with tire irons in their hands] and—since I had a rental car—took the kids swimming to Canton [since the pools in Jackson had been closed]."

SNCC organizers knew that voting wasn't the only key to equality and freedom. Even if they could vote, Mississippians wouldn't rise above poverty if they were poorly educated and oblivious to the outside world. Certainly, the black youth of Mississippi were not properly educated. As mentioned, the state spent four times more money per student on whites than blacks. Textbooks were whitewashed; Reconstruction was not even taught in some school districts.

Volunteer Robert Hargreaves remembered asking two African American teachers what was being taught in the black schools. "They told me that they would be immediately fired if they ever tried to teach the U.S. Constitution!" he wrote.

In the fall of 1963, SNCC Field Secretary Charlie Cobb proposed an alternative learning experience for Mississippi students. His Freedom Schools would "provide an educational experience for students which will make it possible for them to challenge the myths of our society, to perceive more clearly its realities, and to find alternatives, and ultimately, new directions for action."

In March 1964, the National Council of Churches sponsored a meeting in New York City. During discussions, SNCC members, clergy, and educators agreed on a curriculum for the schools. After Staughton Lynd, a history professor at Spellman College, took over as director of the Freedom Schools, the curriculum changed slightly. It included academics, recreation and cultural activities, and leadership development.

In addition to reading, writing, and mathematics, Freedom School students were taught science, debate, dance, and foreign languages. They learned the American history that wasn't included in their textbooks, including black history.

A Freedom School teacher meets with her class on the front steps of Mt. Zion Baptist Church in Hattiesburg, Mississippi. (© *Herbert Randall, McCain Library & Archives, University of Southern Mississippi*)

They were taught about the civil rights movement, especially current events.

"The students were taken seriously in the Freedom Schools," wrote Freedom School coordinator Liz Fusco. "They were encouraged to talk, and their talking was listened to. They were assigned to write, and their writing was read with attention to idea and style as well as to grammar. They were encouraged to sing, to dance, to draw, to play, to laugh."

The Freedom Schools were a resounding success. More than 3,000 students attended, tripling the organizers' initial goal. Freedom School staff members overcame the fears of black parents, the lack of venues for classrooms, and violent retaliation by white locals. In McComb, after whites bombed a church used as a Freedom School, teachers held subsequent classes on the lawn.

Spirit in the communities ran high. In Harmony, people fixed up former schools to use as Freedom Schools. Teachers

An outdoor Freedom School class (© *Herbert Randall, McCain Library & Archives, University of Southern Mississippi*)

expressed a wide range of experiences—from frustration and classroom chaos to energized students showing an unquenchable desire to learn. Volunteer Deborah Rand recalled that "the kids were extraordinary—excited about our presence, eager to learn, and anxious for change. I loved working with them."

"The atmosphere in the class is unbelievable," said Freedom School teacher Pam Parker. "It is what every teacher dreams about—real, honest enthusiasm and desire to learn anything and everything. The girls come to class of their own free will. They respond to everything that is said. They are excited about learning. They drain me of everything that I have to offer so that I go home at night completely exhausted but very happy in spirit."

Students were encouraged to express themselves. In Holly Springs, students wrote and performed a play. Several started student newspapers. Frances Jeffries wrote the top story for *The Freedom News* in the newspaper's Vol. 1, No. 1 edition. "How We Feel About the Three Missing Boys," the headline read. Jeffries reported: "Some say the police are not looking as hard as they should be."

Part of the goal of the curriculum was to implant habits of freethinking and lay groundwork for a statewide youth movement. Older students learned about the white power structure and the fear and guilt—for both whites and blacks—that accompanied it. Even younger students learned some powerful social lessons. "The children were fascinated by 'straight hair' and white skin," wrote teacher Jo Ann Robinson, "and we had endless discussions about why such attributes weren't really 'good' and their own hair and skin were definitely not 'bad' as they insisted."

Some students were fiercely determined to get an education. Teacher Than Porter, who taught remedial mathematics, recalled a boy who walked four miles to attend his classes. Moreover, many black adults eagerly joined the literacy classes that the volunteer teachers provided. Porter recalled a seventy-two-year-old illiterate man who rode a mule to get to school. He also taught an African American man who "was so glad to be able to talk freely to a white man that he talked constantly—so much that I couldn't get a word in edgewise."

Gloria Clark recalled that black senior citizens were determined to learn to read. "I just remember some men who were just adamant," she recalled. "They were going to learn to read at seventy years old so that they could take that test and register to vote. . . . I taught reading to adults at night with a potbelly stove, bad lighting—you know, bad materials."

For many of the teachers, their work during Freedom Summer was the most emotionally powerful experience of their lives. Clark took pride that she taught children to read for the very first time. Elinor Tideman Arthur fondly recalled how black women from the nearby church brought teachers homemade lunch every day. Working and sharing together, blacks and whites enriched all of their lives.

"I learned from them, they learned from me," said Clark. "I let them have whatever strengths and skills I had, and they gave me their strengths and skills, which were considerable. . . . And nobody felt cheated. Nobody felt exploited or overused in one capacity because you grew together and you learned from each other."

eight

The Freedom Party

Not only were SNCC leaders courageous, well organized, and relentless workers, but they were not afraid to think big. It was one thing to canvas neighborhoods to register voters; quite another to force a showdown with Mississippi's Democratic Party on the nation's largest stage.

After the success of the Freedom Vote in the fall of 1963, Bob Moses and SNCC launched the Mississippi Freedom Democratic Party (MFDP) to challenge the state's all-white Democratic Party. Prominent civil rights leaders Bayard Rustin and Ella Baker worked with SNCC as advisers. Moses also convinced white attorney Joseph Rauh, head of the D.C. Democratic Party, to support the MFDP. Committed to justice, Rauh stated that "if there's anybody at the Democratic convention challenging the seating of the outlaw Mississippi Democrats, I'll make sure that the challengers are seated."

The MFDP got off the ground in April 1964, just months before the next presidential election. That month, SNCC opened an office for the party in Washington, D.C., and the MFDP held its first rally in Jackson. Two hundred delegates from across the state attended. The organization's first goal was to place four candidates on the ballot for the Mississippi Democratic primary as delegates to be sent to the Democratic National Convention, which would be held in Atlantic City, New Jersey, that August. In June, Americans for Democratic Action (ADA), for which Rauh served as vice-president, declared that the MFDP delegation—not the racist Democratic Party of Mississippi—should be recognized at the upcoming convention. Democrats in the states of New York and Michigan also endorsed the MFDP delegation.

The new party geared up for a showdown in Atlantic City. In early August, the MFDP attracted more than 2,000 people to a convention and selected a delegation to go to the national convention. Sixty-eight people, including four whites, comprised the delegation. Aaron Henry, Fannie Lou Hamer, and Ed King were among the delegation's leaders. At this point, the MFDP had the support of twenty-five U.S. Congress members as well as delegates from nine states.

This new upstart party captured the attention of President Lyndon Johnson. Although a strong, proactive supporter of civil rights, Johnson did not like the "trouble" that the MFDP was stirring. Delegations from five southern states threatened to walk out of the convention if the Democratic Party's Credentials Committee decided to seat the MFDP delegates instead of the all-white Mississippi delegates. The last thing the President wanted was chaos among his own party, especially with major issues on his agenda: escalation

Aaron Henry speaks before the Credentials Committee at the Democratic National Convention. *(Library of Congress)*

of hostilities in Vietnam, controversial civil rights legislation in Washington, and the presidential election in November.

Johnson enlisted vice-presidential candidate Hubert Humphrey, a liberal Democrat from Minnesota, to talk to Rauh, who served as counsel for the MFDP. "'Joe, just give me something to tell the President,'" Rauh recalled Humphrey saying. "I said, 'Why don't you tell him I'm a dirty bastard and completely uncontrollable?'" With that exchange, it became clear that the MFDP would not retreat meekly back to Mississippi. As Aaron Henry would say later in the month, "We did not come to Atlantic City to get the same kind of back in the bus treatment we have gotten in Mississippi."

The MFDP delegation put its faith in what was called the "eleven-and-eight" procedure. Representatives of the MFDP would first appear before the convention's Credentials Committee, asking if the MFDP delegates could be seated during the convention. All the MFDP reps needed to do was convince eleven of the one hundred-plus committee members to vote for sending the MFDP request to the convention floor.

A vote on the convention floor could be in one of two forms: voice vote or roll-call vote. The MFDP did not want a voice vote since the results of the voting would be deter-mined by the "ears" of those in charge of the convention, who were partisans of President Johnson. To secure the preferred roll-call vote, the MFDP would have to convince eight state delegations to request the roll-call vote.

Fannie Lou Hamers speaks at the 1964 Democratic National Convention. *(Library of Congress)*

On August 22, the first day of the convention, Fannie Lou Hamer pleaded the MFDP's case before the Credentials Committee. Network news crews arrived in force. Hamer, the youngest of twenty children, was the daughter of sharecroppers on a cotton plantation. Though denied a proper education as a child, she now served as vice-chair of the MFDP. Her plainspoken, heartfelt pleas captivated listeners.

Hamer recalled the time she was arrested in June 1963 after attending a voter-registration workshop. While in jail, she heard lawmen beat a woman in a nearby cell. Then they came for Hamer. A state highway patrolman told Fannie Lou, "We are going to make you wish you was dead."

Hamer told the committee that she was told to lay face-down, and that the police ordered an African American man to beat her with a blackjack. "The second Negro began to beat and I began to work my feet, and the state highway patrolman ordered the first Negro who had beat me to sit upon my feet to keep me from working my feet. I began to scream, and one white man got up and began to beat me in my head and told me to hush."

Hamer was reduced to tears, but she continued. "All of this is on account we want to register," she said, "to become first-class citizens. And if the Freedom Democratic Party is not seated now, I question America. Is this America, the land of the free and the home of the brave, where we have to sleep with our telephones off the hooks because our lives be threatened daily, because we want to live as decent human beings—in America?"

President Johnson found Hamer's words so disparaging to the Democratic Party that he abruptly called a news conference, hoping to immediately shift the media's focus. Reporters did go to cover the president, but that night news stations showed long film footage of Hamer's plea. Millions of Americans were outraged.

Working with Minnesota Attorney General Walter Mondale, Humphrey proposed a compromise. According to the proposal, which the White House approved, the white Mississippi Democrats would be seated if they pledged their loyalty to the ticket. Two MFDP delegates, Henry and King, would also get seats at the convention as "at-large" delegates—not officially representing Mississippi. They also put forth a resolution that stated that all future southern Democrat delegations would be integrated.

Although Rauh endorsed the proposal, both the MFDP and the white Democrats disliked it. The MFDP wanted all of its delegates to be seated, not just two. The white Democrats were even more incensed, claiming they would not pledge loyalty to a party that was pushing for integration. In fact, all but three of the white Mississippi delegates left the convention.

Despite both sides' distaste for the proposal, the Credentials Committee voted to approve the compromise. It then went to the convention floor, where it was approved by a voice vote. The deal was done; two at-large seats were all the MFDP would get. Moses was furious, claiming that the white power structure had shafted African Americans yet again. "You cannot trust the political system," he fumed. Hamer stated that two seats was nothing more than tokenism—a meaningless gesture intended solely to keep the black upstarts quiet.

On Tuesday night, the episode turned ugly. Hamer and other MFDP members borrowed passes from sympathetic delegates from other states and entered the convention hall. Then, in total defiance, they sat on the seats vacated by the boycotting white delegates of Mississippi. Johnson responded by having all of the Mississippi chairs removed except for

Seats assigned to Mississippi's delegation at the Democratic National Convention are empty after the all-white delegation from Mississippi decided to leave rather than accept a compromise with the MFDP delegation. *(Courtesy of AP Images)*

three, and those would be reserved for the three white delegates who hadn't left the convention.

The following day, MFDP members met and debated about whether to accept the proposal of two at-large delegates. By accepting it, some argued, they would better ingratiate themselves with Washington lawmakers. Others claimed that acceptance meant appeasement, a sellout, with no real tangible benefit to Mississippi blacks. The members decided to stand tall and proud and reject the proposal.

On Wednesday evening, MFDP members again borrowed passes and crashed the convention. Since Mississippi seats had been removed, they stood in the spaces were the chairs once were. A reporter asked Hamer if she wanted equality with the white man. "What would I look like fighting for equality with the white man?" she retorted. "I don't want to go down that low. I want true democracy that'll raise the white man up—raise America up."

For those who desired immediate results, MFDP's efforts in Atlantic City were disappointing, as the all-white political power structure remained intact. However, this new Freedom party shook the established order. MFDP members made a powerful statement on the national stage, and they won the hearts of American citizens, including many members of Congress.

In January 1965, MFDP members went to Washington, where they challenged the seating of Mississippi's five representatives. The House even took a vote to see if the MFDP candidates should be seated, and 149 representatives (out of 475 who participated) voted yes.

At various points in 1964, SNCC staffers, the summer volunteers, local citizens, and the MFDP grew frustrated

This edition of the *Student Voice*, a newspaper produced by SNCC, gives an account of the MFDP campaign. *(Courtesy of Zoya Zeman Papers, McCain Library & Archives, University of Southern Mississippi)*

with their civil rights efforts. What good is a few registered voters, a summer's worth of freedom schooling, or a grandstanding event in New Jersey? Their individual deeds may have seemed small, but their collective efforts were—slowly but surely—fomenting a revolution. As those 149 representatives cast a vote of support for the MFDP, it became clear that the southern white caste system was on the verge of destruction. Fannie Lou Hamer would one day achieve her dream of a true democracy.

nine
Violence and Tension

Missippi Burning—MIBURN—was the FBI's code-name for the firebombing and violence that con-stituted white Mississippians' terror campaign against civil rights workers.

"I really cannot describe how sick I think this state is," wrote volunteer Michael Kenney. "When I walk I am always looking at cars and people: if Negro, they are my friends; if white, I am frightened and walk faster. When driving, I am always asking: black? white? It is the fear and uncertainty that is maddening."

Throughout the summer, COFO staffers compiled a daily record of hostile incidents across the state. From June 20 through August 26, they recorded such episodes every single day. A typical day included a half-dozen reported incidents; some days had ten or more. Below are four of the ten reports on August 12:

> **Greenwood:** Six local Negro youths arrested today while standing in front of Doris' store in Baptist Town, singing. At least one beaten.
> **Ruleville:** Mrs. Hamer threatened with murder in telephone call to her home tonight.
> **Ocean Springs (near Gulfport):** In two separate incidents, two local Negro men shot at here today.
> **Brandon:** St. Matthews Baptist Church here burned to ground last night.

The overall numbers were staggering: In addition to the Chaney-Goodman-Schwerner triple murder, another activist was killed and four were critically injured. Eighty people were beaten and roughly a thousand were arrested. Thirty-seven churches were burned or bombed, as were thirty homes and businesses.

Many volunteers and activists were involved in multiple incidents. Stated Frank Cieciorka, "I was beaten once, involved in high-speed chases twice, and jailed four times." As SNCC leader Stokely Carmichael liked to say, "If anyone isn't paranoid around here, they're crazy!"

Volunteer David Gelfand, who lived with a black family in Meridian, narrowly averted death. For days, the family had received threatening phone calls, and the family feared that their car might be rigged with explosives. They even went so far as to tape a single hair across the opening of the car's hood. If it was broken, it meant that someone had opened the hood in order to plant explosives. One morning, the home's owner noticed that the hair was indeed broken.

"And the carport was right next to the kids' bedroom—ages four to twelve," Gelfand recalled. "And so he said, 'Okay, let's not do anything but release the emergency break and roll it out to the road.' And we did that and then opened the hood. And there were four sticks of dynamite tied [to] . . . the ignition coil."

According to volunteer Deborah Rand, women and children were not off-limits. "During a meeting that SNCC held at a church, carloads of whites drove by and shot into the meeting, injuring a young black woman," Rand remembered. "As I walked down the street with my Freedom School students, cars swerved trying to hit us."

In countless cases, civil service workers failed to come to the aid of those in need. "I stayed in a . . . freedom house of a wonderful woman, Ms. McGruder, who housed and fed us," wrote volunteer Spes Dolphin. "Eventually her house was firebombed, and the insurance refused to pay. The fire company came and watched the house burn. Other places were burned the same night."

Freedom Summer volunteers David Owen (left) and Lawrence Spears (right) stand with Rabbi Arthur J. Lelyveld (middle) on the day after all three were attacked and beaten. (© Herbert Randall, McCain Library & Archives, University of Southern Mississippi)

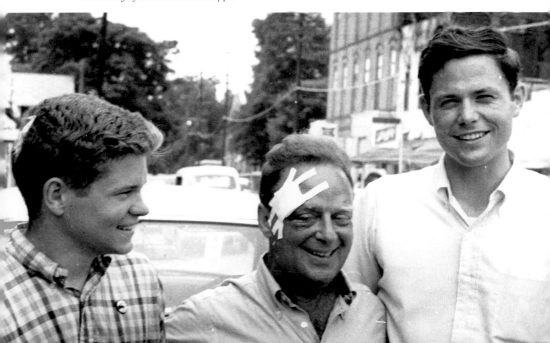

In another incident, local activist Silas McGhee of Greenwood was shot in the head. Three volunteers took off their shirts and tied them around McGhee's wound to stop the bleeding. When they arrived at the hospital, they were told that McGhee couldn't be admitted because the volunteers weren't wearing shirts.

To counteract the atrocities, a "cavalry" of lawyers, doctors, and clergy participated in Freedom Summer. One hundred and fifty lawyers volunteered, one of whom—after spending time in the state—compared Mississippi to Nazi Germany. Joining the lawyers were a hundred doctors, nurses, and psychiatrists from the Medical Committee for Human Rights. From the National Council of Churches, four hundred priests, ministers, and rabbis arrived to tend to spiritual needs.

The presence of the northern media and the FBI also benefited the Project workers and local black citizens. Local whites thought twice about committing a major crime with so many reporters and federal agents snooping around. According to Fannie Lou Hamer, the typical white perpetrator was nothing but cowardly. "Out in the daylight, he don't do nothin'," she said. "But at night, he'll toss a bomb or pay someone to kill. The white man's afraid he'll be treated like he's been treatin' Negroes . . . ."

Meanwhile, the Summer Projects' Communications Office was outstanding at acquiring and disseminating information about violent incidents. SNCC was also clever about public relations. If a volunteer was arrested or beaten, SNCC thought it smart to contact the volunteer's hometown newspaper. As the summer unfolded and attacks occurred at an alarming rate, SNCC found that it didn't have the manpower for such PR.

This volunteer points to a bullet hole in the front of a car that was parked outside of a local civil rights leader's business. (© *Herbert Randall, McCain Library & Archives, University of Southern Mississippi*)

However, soon after Schwerner, Goodman, and Chaney disappeared, COFO staffers sent letters to all of the volunteers' parents asking them to pressure politicians to protect Project workers and to alert their local media. Many parents organized support groups, including the Parents Mississippi Emergency Committee and the Parents Summer Project Support Organization. Such groups raised funds and lobbied in Washington.

With so many of the volunteers hailing from prominent, wealthy families, some of the parents had enough clout to influence Washington's decision-makers. In fact, at least a few parents were federal "big-wigs." Both Congressman Don Edwards (D-CA) and Arthur Schlesinger, Jr., who had been a close aide of the president in the Kennedy administration, had children working as Project volunteers.

SNCC's plan to attract well-off volunteers worked beautifully. Every time a Klansman bombed a church or beat an activist, it made influential Northerners angrier and more determined to push for justice in the Jim Crow South.

In previous years in Mississippi, retaliatory terror had seemed to work for whites. After several African Americans were lynched in that state in 1955, including Emmett Till,

Peter Werner, a graduate student at the University of Michigan and Freedom Summer worker, talks on the phone after having been attacked while walking in downtown Hattiesburg, Mississippi. (© *Herbert Randall, McCain Library & Archives, University of Southern Mississippi*)

black citizens remained very much "in line." In fact, a White Citizens' Council reported in 1957 that Mississippi had "not one single school suit, or bus suit; and all is peaceful and serene with regard to race relations."

But thanks to SNCC, this was a much different Mississippi in 1964. No matter how much violence whites unleashed, the citizenry pushed forward. "My grandmother was afraid," a black Mississippi woman was quoted as saying in July 1964. "My mother was afraid. But I'm not afraid and my children aren't afraid. They use terror to make us afraid, but one day they will have to stop because if we're not afraid, what will be the use of their terror?"

In the midst of the violence, black citizens and volunteers became "brothers in arms." Teacher David Gass remembered when his Freedom School was burned. "At a mass meeting," he wrote, "a frail, old woman in a sharecropper hat said: 'I want ten men, none of them crippled. Bring your guns. We gonna form a Deacons for Defense and rebuild that school.' We sang the songs that ring in my ears today."

Sally Belfrage recalled the day in Greenwood when police arrested a large group of black voter applicants and white volunteers, including herself. As they were marched into a bus (a makeshift paddy wagon), the activists chanted "Freedom! Freedom!" and sang "Ain't Gonna Let Nobody Turn Me Around."

Inside the bus, Belfrage wrote, a "frail old woman beat an umbrella on the floor in time. . . . 'FREEDOM! FREEDOM! FREEDOM! FREEDOM!' The shout ripped the air apart as we drove off, building a wild elation and sense of power."

Belfrage's experience epitomized the "freedom high" that so many of the Project workers felt. "Everyone experienced a 'freedom high,'" wrote Deborah Rand. "We felt we were the lucky few. We were part of a movement that would transform the country. We had the privilege of working for justice, of being on the side of 'right,' and it made us high."

Conversely, the unstable mix of blacks and whites, poor and privileged, did generate a great deal tension among the local African Americans and volunteers. Moreover, the ever-present dangers, difficult work, overcrowded homes, and stifling heat further strained relationships. Many SNCC workers resented the national attention heaped on the volunteers. African Americans had suffered in Mississippi since the 1700s, but only now—when the white kids came—did anyone seem to care. And would anyone care once the whites left?

In addition, some white volunteers acted paternalistically. This was not unexpected. To a large extent, white Americans felt a great deal of bravado during this era. They had won the war in the 1940s and, in the 1950s, generated the most-advanced economy in world history. The U.S. felt it could impose its will in such nonwhite regions as Central America and Southeast Asia.

In the early '60s, white youths attended college in record numbers. *Time* magazine would name the "Under-25 generation" its "Man of the Year" for 1966, with a white male's face dominating the cover. As high-achieving college students, volunteers—at least some of them—had an elevated opinion of themselves. One white female volunteer groused about the incompetence of the black COFO staff members. "Several times I've had to completely re-do press statements or letters written by one of them," she complained. She then added that she had to "overlook or purposely and pointedly misinterpret their occasional thrusts of antagonism."

Sexual tension was also a big issue. Activists could talk all they wanted to about their "beloved community." However, when black men slept with white female volunteers, white men and black women quietly seethed.

Tensions arose over seemingly trivial issues. The challenges of oppressed blacks and privileged whites was made explicit in "who took out the garbage," wrote Kay Michener. "Black students did not want to do something menial which had been their traditional role. Neither did women. The white men felt that they should not be stuck with all the cleanup. Dirt and garbage piled up."

Fortunately for all involved, blacks and whites overcame most of their differences. Regarding the garbage situation, Michener wrote, SNCC leader Stokely Carmichael "came

Although there were times of racial tension among volunteers during the Summer Project, most of the workers came to feel closely bonded to each other. (© *Herbert Randall, McCain Library & Archives, University of Southern Mississippi*)

to the rescue. Stokely was so loved and respected by everyone that when he took out the garbage and began cleaning, everyone pitched in and the place stayed clean. Such is the stuff of leadership."

Rand believed that SNCC workers' resentment gradually faded away. "They had been beaten and arrested," she stated. "Friends had been killed. They were angry that America was not 'America' for them. Nevertheless, once the SNCC staff found that we worked hard and got along with the community, they were protective and caring."

Unita Blackwell, a black SNCC worker, treasured her new relationships. "There was interaction of blacks and whites," she said. "I remember cooking some pinto beans—that's all we had—and everybody just got around the pot . . . sitting on the floor, sitting anywhere . . . and they was talking and we was sitting there laughing, and I guess they became very real and very human, we each to one another. It was an experience that will last a lifetime."

Added Michener: "We shelled peas, held babies, and attended lots of church mass meetings at which we always heard the remark, 'You are the first white folk who ever called me Mr. or Mrs.' I experienced the Black community as a loving, friendly, comfortable place to be."

By late August, with fall approaching, Freedom Summer activities wound down. About a third of the volunteers didn't leave, choosing to remain in Mississippi and continue to fight for justice in various roles. But most of the volunteers returned to their homes and universities. Goodbyes were difficult and emotional. Many summer recruits felt guilty leaving their "war buddies," the black activists, behind. Bonds were so strong that more than thirty marriages would occur among volunteers—some interracial.

As they arrived "home" in their comfortable suburbs or on their peaceful campuses, volunteers felt strangely out of place. Why were the neighborhoods so pleasant? Why was conversation so banal? Many returnees felt disoriented, depressed, alienated. Some, including Michener, claimed feelings of paranoia. "I had to get used to not regarding all whites as out to do me harm and stop looking for guns in passing cars," she wrote.

Volunteer Len Edward found it difficult to relate to people once he returned to law school. "[S]uddenly I'm back reading law books again," he wrote, "and sitting with guys drinking beer and they want to talk about how the Cubs are doing and talk b.s. and talk about girls and somebody casually says, 'well, what was happening down there in Mississippi?' . . . And I started talking and I said about two sentences and I started crying; I just burst out crying and it wasn't just . . . a little trickle down the cheek. . . . I just sobbed."

ten

The Impact of Freedom Summer

Though Freedom Summer ended in late August 1964, its influence, both on the state of society and the people who worked so hard in their fight against injustice, carried on well past the coming of fall.

The statewide movement continued, thanks largely to the leadership of tiny Liz Fusco, the tireless Freedom School coordinator. A "what's happening" report issued in late September indicated a flurry of activity across the state, including: school for children and adults in Ruleville, voter-registration classes in Mound Bayou, a theater group and citizenship seminars in Meridian, and college prep courses in Greenwood. Other activists worked to establish food banks, day care centers, and farming cooperatives.

One of SNCC's dreams, fostering leadership among the youth of Mississippi, came true in August, when a group of high school students formed the Mississippi Student Union (MSU). The MSU began with a convention that month and kept on going. Politically active, they passed resolutions asking for the enforcement of the Civil Rights Act of 1964, the elimination of the poll tax, and other reforms. In local communities, they tutored black students and pushed for school integration.

Activist Jerry Von Korff missed Freedom Summer, but he and others wanted to help that fall after a church was burned down in Ripley, Mississippi. "At Oberlin [College] . . . with the blessing of COFO, we organized Carpenters for Christmas, a drive to rebuild the Ripley Church," he wrote. "We organized a national fund raising drive. That Christmas we celebrated Christmas in a church built with volunteer labor."

After largely ignoring the plight of black Mississippians for decades, the federal government finally lent a helping hand in the wake of the Summer Project. Federal money poured into the state for schools, nutrition programs, legal aid, and health clinics. The national Project Head Start evolved from Freedom Summer; by 2005, more than 20 million young children had benefited from Head Start, which has provided education, nutrition, and health services to low-income children and their families.

The federal courts also interceded in Mississippi. In several counties, federal courts issued injunctions against white school officials, ordering them to integrate their schools. In the 1967 court case *United States v. Cecil Price, et al.,* eighteen men went on trial for conspiring to murder Michael Schwerner, James Chaney, and Andrew Goodman. Despite an all-white jury in Meridian, Mississippi, seven of the men were convicted, including Cecil Price, the chief deputy sheriff of Neshoba County, and Sam H. Bowers, Jr., the imperial wizard of the White Knights of the Ku Klux Klan.

Deputy Sheriff Cecil Price (left) is escorted by FBI agents to be arraigned on conspiring to murder Michael Schwerner, James Chaney, and Andrew Goodman. *(Courtesy of AP Images/Horace Cort)*

In late June, the disappearance of the three civil rights workers rocked Washington. At the time, the Civil Rights Bill of 1964 had just passed the Senate (on June 19), and President Johnson signed it into law on July 2. Addressing America that day, President Johnson's speech reflected the spirit of Freedom Summer: "This Civil Rights Act is a challenge to all of us to go to work in our communities and our states, in our homes and in our hearts, to eliminate the last vestiges of injustice in our beloved country."

The Civil Rights Act would prove effective at ending segregation in public facilities in the South. However, it lacked the enforcement power to end voting injustice. But through the publicity generated by the Summer Project, as well as SNCC's and other civil rights groups' epic protests in Selma, Alabama, Congress passed the Voting Rights Act of 1965.

The act banned biased literacy tests and other exclusionary screening devices used by registrars to keep black citizens from registering. The act also allowed federal workers to register black voters when necessary.

Freedom Summer volunteer Robert Hargreaves pointed out that Summer Project efforts contributed directly to the 1965 act. "In order to register to vote, the applicant had to pass a four-page test that included interpreting a section of the Mississippi constitution selected by the registrar," Hargreaves wrote. "Passing or failing was completely at the discretion of the registrar with no explanation. All summer we were taking people to the courthouse to register, but to my knowledge no one ever passed. A big part of the summer project was to document this. This was presented to Congress and was a major influence in passing the Voting Rights Act."

The 1965 act was extraordinarily effective in ending voting injustice. On the very day after Johnson signed the act into law, the U.S. Justice Department filed suit against the use of the poll tax in Mississippi. On August 7, U.S. Attorney General Nicholas Katzenbach's office began notifying officials in the Deep South that all "tests and devices" related to voter-registration were invalid.

On August 10, examiners with the Civil Service Commission began registering black citizens to vote in nine southern counties. By late October, they had processed 56,000 black registrants. Local officials in Mississippi and other Deep South states registered thousands more black citizens. In 1964, only 6.7 percent of Mississippi's voting-age blacks had registered to vote—16.3 percent below the national average. By 1969, that number leaped to 66.5 percent—5.5 percent above the national average. The courageous efforts of SNCC,

CORE, the Freedom Summer volunteers, and of course the black citizens of Mississippi had paid off. The voter-registration movement was a resounding success.

All the while, SNCC was beset with internal strife. Originally, SNCC leaders had the same core beliefs as Martin Luther King Jr. Through nonviolent protests, they hoped to appeal to the consciousness of America and federal leaders. Their ultimate goal was integration. As the 1960s progressed, however, SNCC members lost much of their idealism—and it was easy to see why. Whites had beaten activists mercilessly on the Freedom Rides in 1961, and numerous other protests (not to mention the provocations during Freedom Summer) also led to physical assault and incarceration.

Entering Freedom Summer, SNCC members were angry with federal officials, who had done little to help the civil rights cause and protect movement protesters. Even SNCC's master plan for the Summer Project included an element of white hostility, as SNCC tried to attract national attention by subjecting the rich white students to physical assault. The events in Atlantic City caused many in SNCC to completely lose their faith in the white system. Even President Johnson, supposedly a friend of the movement, made it clear that the MFDP was not welcome at the national convention.

Black-white tensions were exacerbated after Freedom Summer when more than eighty white volunteers joined SNCC, nearly equaling the number of black SNCC members. Most of these white volunteers were women, and some of them had intimate relationships with SNCC men—a situation that infuriated the black women of SNCC. Sarah Evans, in her book *Personal Politics,* wrote that some of SNCC's black women complained that they "could not develop relationships with the black men because the men didn't have to be responsible to them because they could always hook up with some white woman who had come down." White men were not terribly welcomed in SNCC either, as blacks felt that they exhibited paternalism and dominance, which stifled the development of SNCC staff members.

Emotions aside, SNCC leaders debated the philosophy of integrated versus all-black membership. Those committed to SNCC's original goals advocated continued community projects, such as citizenship seminars and food banks—in which case, a racial mix of project workers would be acceptable. However, another faction of SNCC felt it was time for SNCC to build a national political power base. They thought it naive for African Americans to expect the white powers of Washington to bestow opportunities upon them. They believed that a large black political coalition was needed to fight for black rights.

This philosophical debate raged within SNCC throughout the mid-1960s and caused divisions within the organization. On June 17, 1966, newly elected SNCC Chairman Stokely Carmichael revved up the crowd in Greenwood, Mississippi, with cries of "Black Power." On December 1, 1966, SNCC ruled to exclude white activists from its membership.

As SNCC switched to a black power—some have argued militant—organization, the whole civil rights movement steered in that direction as well. This was especially true in America's large cities, where black citizens wallowed in poverty, were excluded from certain jobs, and were victims of police brutality.

The phrase "Long, Hot Summer," which had applied to Freedom Summer in 1964, also was bestowed on the middle months of 1967. Black insurrections raged in many major northern cities, resulting in approximately a hundred deaths and thousands of injuries. SNCC didn't directly cause the rioting, of course, but some argued that its rhetoric contributed to it. On July 25, 1967, in a speech in Cambridge, Maryland, new SNCC Chairman H. Rap Brown proclaimed, "If America don't come around,

H. Rap Brown *(Library of Congress)*

we're going to burn it down." After the speech, rioting ensued throughout the city.

The Black Power movement dramatically affected the nation. Richard Nixon was elected president in 1968 on a "law and order" platform. In such major cities as Detroit and Cleveland, whites moved out of the suburbs largely because of the black insurrections that had occurred in their cities. These whites took with them their substantial incomes, leaving the cities with low tax bases. These cities became impoverished, and black ghetto life became more entrenched in the 1970s and beyond.

A demonstrator stands on top of a campus police car and addresses a crowd during 1964 student protests on the Berkeley campus. *(Courtesy of AP Images)*

In addition to SNCC, Freedom Summer had a strong impact on the Free Speech Movement (FSM) that emerged at the University of California-Berkeley in the fall of 1964. Berkeley was well known for its liberalism, but during that fall semester, a new school policy prohibited students from setting up tables on campus to promote "off-campus" causes, such as civil rights. The faculty-student conflict reached a crescendo on October 1, when a police car was soon surrounded by 3,000 students chanting civil rights songs. On December 2, police arrested 770 student protesters.

The university decided to give in to the students' demands. It was a defining moment of the era—a great victory for the anti-Establishment youth of the '60s. Mario Savio, the most celebrated leader of the Free Speech Movement, had drawn his inspiration from his work in the Mississippi Summer Project. "Last summer I went to Mississippi to join the struggle there for civil rights," Savio said. "This fall I am engaged in another phase of the same struggle, this time in Berkeley."

One Freedom Summer volunteer who knew Savio insisted that there was "no way he [Savio] ever would have . . . stepped forward [at Berkeley] if it hadn't been for Mississippi." Though normally shy, the volunteer said, Savio developed character during the Summer Project: "There was this single-mindedness of purpose and moral certainty that just pushed him . . . and it came from Mississippi, I think."

Above all, the 1960s were known for student radicalism. On college campuses across the nation, America's youth railed against the Establishment. It was the era of the New Left, long hair, hippies, the counterculture, the Generation Gap, draft dodging, and massive student protests. Of course, the Vietnam War was the major event that alienated youth. Young men saw themselves as sacrificial lambs, drafted and inducted into the Army against their will and shipped to faraway jungles, where they died by the thousands for what they believed was a purposeless war.

Yet while the war antagonized and alienated white youth, so too did Freedom Summer. The white volunteers who worked on the Summer Project, who absorbed SNCC leadership's powerful messages, were appalled by American hypocrisy and injustice. How could the U.S. call itself a "beacon of democracy" in Southeast Asia and Central America when it allowed its own citizens to be assaulted simply for trying to vote? How could the wealthiest nation in the world allow its own people, such as the African Americans in Mississippi, to live in extreme poverty?

The volunteers, many of whom had been JFK-inspired idealists, became far more cynical after Freedom Summer. A survey revealed that they emerged with less respect for the president, Congress, the U.S. Justice Department, and the FBI. Moreover, through television and newspapers, students across the country learned about the injustices in Mississippi during Freedom Summer. The media also hailed volunteers as heroes, making them role models for other young liberals.

Freedom Summer veterans and energized college students returned to their campuses with an activist spirit. Said volunteer David Gass, "The heroism I saw in Mississippi inspired me to become involved in the major antiwar demonstrations, the Cleveland riots in '68, [and the] Kent State episode."

With the war heating up in 1964 and '65, and student activists highly energized, movements sprouted on campuses. As at Berkeley, Freedom Summer veterans were often at the forefront. After being drafted, former volunteer Bruce Maxwell made an antiwar statement by burning his induction papers.

At the University of Michigan in March 1965, the first of the many teach-ins took place. In the spirit of the SNCC sit-ins of the early 1960s, the teach-ins were mass gatherings of students and faculty, forums to learn about and debate the many facets of the Vietnam War, but they in effect served as mass demonstrations against the war. It is no coincidence that the teach-in was born at the University of Michigan since some of the student organizers had been volunteers of SNCC's Summer Project. Also, a faculty organizer had been a CORE member who had established a Freedom School in Boston.

Other activists who had worked in Mississippi played large roles in the antiwar effort. Sandra Adickes and Norma Becker organized the Teachers Committee for Peace in Vietnam, which took out a full-page ad in the *New York Times* urging the president to end the fighting in Vietnam. In 1967, many Freedom Summer veterans joined fellow antiwar activists in organizing the Vietnam Summer Project, which was based on the Mississippi Summer Project. Hundreds of staff members and thousands of volunteers worked to spread antiwar sentiment throughout the nation.

Freedom Summer volunteers also influenced another '60s crusade—the women's movement. Casey Hayden and Mary King had served in Mississippi during the Summer Project. In 1966 they penned an essay that focused on sexism within the movement and sexism in society in general. The essay, entitled "A Kind of Memo," was highly influential at the time. "It was stunning in its effect on me," one woman stated. "I read it and reread it, and shared it with all my friends. Eventually we started a group in Washington and met on a regular basis to discuss the issues." That fall, a group of women's rights activists formed the National Organization for Women, which would become the largest feminist organization in the world.

When SNCC leaders had first discussed Freedom Summer in the fall of 1963, they never dreamed the Project would evolve into such a phenomenon. In addition to contributing to the death of Jim Crow, the summer experience empowered volunteers to change the world. "A few became lifelong radicals," wrote Jonathan Steele. "None remained untouched."

The legacy of the Summer Project workers extended well past the 1960s. Volunteer Stephen Blum became a pioneer of Upward Bound, a still-thriving program that teaches low-income high school students the skills they need to make it to college. SNCC leader Bob Moses founded the Algebra Project, which helps inner-city and rural students achieve math literacy. In 1981, volunteer Barney Frank was elected to Congress, where he currently ranks as the senior Democrat on the Financial Services Committee.

Volunteer Heather Tobis Booth became co-director of Citizen Action, a progressive political organization with 1.5

Congressman Barney Frank *(Courtesy of AP Images/Susan Walsh)*

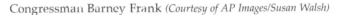

million members. Booth's efforts in 2000 nearly changed the course of the entire world. That year, she was hired as the founding director of the NAACP National Voter Fund, which ran a voter empowerment effort. The campaign helped to increase turnout of African Americans (the great majority of whom were Democrats) by nearly 4.5 million votes over 1996 levels.

"[I]f you organize for justice and a better society, you really can change the world," Booth wrote. "We have changed the world. And we still need to change it for the better." Volunteer Than Porter had a similar message. "Although I was never a leader," he wrote, "I joined several groups like the NAACP, CORE, and some churches. . . . My role was like a snowflake in a blizzard, but remember that without snowflakes there is no blizzard."

But the true influence of Freedom Summer, the true benefit and legacy of it lies with the people whose lives so many worked to improve. Larry Taylor, a black man who grew up in Como, Mississippi in the 1950s, spent his life surrounded by injustice, oppression, cruelty, and the stern voice of authority constantly proclaiming that he, and those like him, were second class, inferior. But that hot summer in 1964 changed everything. "After Freedom Summer," he wrote, "for the first time in my life, I felt like an American."

Timeline

1960	April	The Student Nonviolent Coordinating Committee (SNCC) emerges in North Carolina.
	August	SNCC worker Marion Barry teaches nonviolent protest methods to black teenagers in Mississippi.
	Sept. 25	African American Herbert Lee is murdered by E. H. Hurst, a local white legislator, for trying to register to vote in McComb County, Mississippi.
1962		The Council of Federated Organizations (COFO), comprised mostly of SNCC members is organized to coordinate voter registration in the South.
1963	June 12	NAACP Field Director Medgar Evers is assassinated at his home in Jackson, Mississippi, by white supremacist Byron de la Beckwith.
	July	Allard Lowenstein of New York proposes the idea of a mock election in Mississippi.
	Nov. 7:	Through SNCC's efforts, more than 90,000 black citizens cast "freedom ballots" in mock election in Mississippi.

1964 January: The COFO staff approves a plan for the Mississippi Summer Project; northern college-age students commit to help COFO staff members register black Mississippians and run "Freedom Schools." .

April 26 SNCC members form the Mississippi Freedom Democratic Party (MFDP) as alternative Democratic Party in Mississippi.

June 14–27 Hundreds of volunteers—mostly well-off, white Northerners from prestigious universities—attend Mississippi Summer Project orientation in Oxford, Ohio.

June 20–21 Two hundred and fifty voter-registration volunteers arrive by bus in Mississippi.

June 21 Activists James Chaney, Andrew Goodman, and Michael Schwerner disappear on their way back from investigating a burned church.

June 23 An abandoned station wagon, driven by the three missing civil rights workers, is found in a swamp near Philadelphia, Mississippi.

July 2 President Lyndon Johnson signs Civil Rights Act of 1964.

July 10 FBI director J. Edgar Hoover opens an FBI office in Jackson, Mississippi.

Aug. 4: Corpses of James Chaney, Andrew Goodman, and Michael Schwerner are found under an earthen dam near Philadelphia, Mississippi.

Aug.	
22–27	The Mississippi Freedom Democratic Party (MFDP) asks that its delegates—rather than the regular Mississippi Democratic Party delegates — be seated at the Democratic National Convention; MFDP representative Fannie Lou Hamer pleads her case on national television; MFDP rejects Democratic Party's rule that only two at-large seats will be given; MFDP members crash the convention.
1965 Aug. 6	President Johnson signs the Voting Rights Act of 1965.
Aug. 7	Office of U.S. Attorney General Nicholas Katzenbach notifies officials in southern states that all "tests and devices" related to voter registration are invalid.
October	Examiners with the Civil Service Commission have processed 56,000 black registrants.
1966 June 17	SNCC Chairman Stokely Carmichael introduces the organization's message of "Black Power" at a rally in Greenwood, Mississippi.
Dec. 1	SNCC rules to exclude white activists from its membership.
1967 Oct. 20	Seven men are convicted of conspiracy in the 1964 murder of James Chaney, Andrew Goodman, and Michael Schwerner.
1969	More than 66 percent of African Americans in Mississippi were registered to vote.

Sources

CHAPTER ONE: Preface to a Long, Hot Summer

p. 10-11, "Mama, I believe . . . " Sanford Wexler, *An Eyewitness History to the Civil Rights Movement* (New York: Checkmark Books, 1999), 206.

p. 11, "I've got vengeance . . . " Juan Williams, *Eyes on the Prize* (New York: Penguin Books, 1987), 240.

p. 12, "Many say Mississippi . . . " Wexler, *An Eyewitness History*, 208.

p. 12, "[T]his is going . . . " Ibid., 207.

p. 12-13, "Believe me, there . . . " Chris Williams, interview with the author, September 11, 2006.

p. 13, "were adult . . . " Gloria Xifaras Clark, interview with Wilbur Colom, Mississippi Oral History Program, McCaim Library and Archives, University of Southern Mississippi, December 12, 1995, tape 6A and 6B.

p. 13, "We're tired of . . . " Clayborne Carson, primary consultant, *Civil Rights Chronicle: The African-American Struggle for Freedom* (Lincolnwood, Ill.: Legacy Publishing, 2003), 277.

p. 13, "In the summer . . . " Chris Williams, unpublished personal essay, "Murder in Mississippi," June 13, 2005.

CHAPTER TWO: Jim Crow's Stranglehold

p. 14, "What are you eating. . . from the dirt," Patti

Miller's personal Web site, "Dirt," *Keeping History Alive*, http://www.keepinghistoryalive.com/book-excerpts. html.

p. 15, "What you were . . . " Clark, interview.

p. 15, "I think the . . . " Sally Belfrage, *Freedom Summer* (Greenwich, Conn.: Fawcett Publications, 1965), 91.

p. 15, "Where I grew . . . " Larry Taylor, interview with author, September 14, 2006.

p. 17, "no one wants . . . " Belfrage, *Freedom Summer*, 179.

p. 17, "He was a . . . " Deborah Rand, interview with author, September 9, 2006.

p. 17, "backward, dull, imbecilic . . . " Len Holt, *The Summer That Didn't End* (New York: Da Capo Press), 102.

p. 18, "We had hand-me-down . . . " Taylor, interview.

p. 19, "I went to . . . " Belfrage, *Freedom Summer*, 100.

p. 20, "An old black . . . " Robert Hargreaves, interview with author, September 12, 2006.

p. 20, "Do not let . . . " Nicolaus Mills, *Like a Holy Crusade* (Chicago: Elephant Paperbacks, 1993), 45.

p. 21, "There shall be . . . " Lizza Cozzens, "Mississippi & Freedom Summer," The Web site of Robert N.M. Watson, *Watson.org*, 1997, http://www.watson.org/~lisa/blackhistory/civilrights-5565/missippi.html.

p. 23-24, "While in Walthall . . . " John W. Hardy, *Civil Rights Movement Veterans*: *Veterans Roll Call*, http://www.crmvet.org/vet/hardyj.htm.

p. 24, "Do not listen . . . " Williams, *Eyes on the Prize,* 219.

p. 25, "a city of . . . " Ibid., 220.

CHAPTER THREE: Northern Whites Join the Fight

p. 30, "If we're going . . . " Mills, *Like a Holy Crusade*, 64.

p. 30, "[T]hese students bring . . . " Doug McAdam, *Freedom*

Summer (New York: Oxford University Press, 1988), 40.

p. 31, "Emmett Till was . . . " Heather Tobis Booth, interview with author, September 10, 2006.

p. 32, "I have always . . . " Deborah Rand, *Civil Rights Movement Veterans: Veterans Roll Call*, http://www.crmvet.org/vet/randd.htm.

p. 32, "I saw a . . . " Kay Michener, interview with author, October 5, 2006.

p. 33, "I remember his . . . " Clark, interview.

p. 33, "new generation of leadership, " John F. Kennedy, the American Presidency Project, Web site of John Woolley and Gerhard Peters at the University of California, Santa Barbara, http://www.presidency.ucsb.edu/ws/index.php?pid=25966.

p. 34, "[A]re we to . . . " *Encyclopedia Britannica Online*, s.v. "John F. Kennedy: The American Promise to African Americans," http://www.britannica.com/presidents/article-9116924.

p. 35, "'Freeing the Negroes . . . " McAdam, *Freedom Summer*, 20.

p. 35, "The Mississippi Summer . . . " Mills, *Like a Holy Crusade*, 67.

p. 35, "was quite frightened . . . " Booth, interview.

p. 35, "We used to . . . " Bruce Hartford, interview with author, September 8, 2006.

CHAPTER FOUR: Preparing for Battle

p. 39, "Christ called us . . . " McAdam, *Freedom Summer*, 48.

p. 39, "My parents, who . . . " Booth, interview.

p. 40, "Bob Moses made . . . " Williams, interview.

p. 41, "Don't come to . . . " kainah, "Storytime Presents: In Freedom Summer's Footsteps," *Daily Kos Online*,

Web site of Markos Moulitsas,http://www.dailykos. com/story//2007/4/6/213017/7430.

p. 41, "Although you may . . . " Wexler, *An Eyewitness History,* 208.

p. 41, "I may be . . . " Williams, *Eyes on the Prize*, 230.

p. 41, "I was mostly . . . " Frank Cieciorka, interview with author, September 10, 2006.

p. 41-42, "They tend to . . . " Mills, *Like a Holy Crusade*, 88.

p. 42, "There is no . . . " Douglas O. Linder, "Bending Toward Justice: John Doar and the Mississippi Burning Trial," *Mississippi Law Journal*, 72, no. 2 (Winter 2002), http://www.law.umkc.edu/faculty/projects/ ftrials/trialheroes/doaressay.html.

p. 43, "Mississippians Not Going . . . " Mills, *Like a Holy Crusade*, 107.

p. 43, "Outsiders who come . . . " Wexler, *An Eyewitness History,* 206.

p. 43, "They are not . . . " Williams, *Eyes on the Prize*, 229.

p. 44, "she got on stage . . . " Hargreaves, interview.

p. 45, "We're moving the . . . " McAdam, *Freedom Summer*, 71.

p. 45, "Stunned, I walked . . . " Ibid.

p. xx, "Kids were hanging . . . " Mills, *Like a Holy Crusade*, 103.

p. 45-46, "As the bus . . . to my stomach" Patti Miller's personal Web site, "Living with Dying," *Keeping History Alive*, http://www. keepinghistoryalive.com/ book-excerpts3.html.

p. 46, "Bob Moses was . . . " Kay Michener, interview with author, October 5, 2006.

p. 46, "quiet voices broke . . . " Ibid.

p. 46, "Suddenly, I felt . . . " Miller, "Living with Dying."

CHAPTER FIVE: Welcome to Mississippi

p. 47, "When we saw . . . " K.C. Jaehnig, "Freedom Summer volunteer recounts tense times," *Southern Illinois University*, February 5, 2002, http://www.siu.edu/~anthro/adams/pages/news_service_fs.html.

p. 47, "The Greyhound bus . . . " Hargreaves, interview.

p. 48, "The day I . . . " Karen Jo Koonan, interview with author, September 9, 2006.

p. 48, "My first Mississippi . . . " Jonathan Steele, "Summer of Hate," *Guardian,* June 18, 2004.

p. 48, "They took us . . . " Joseph Keesecker, interview with author, September 11, 2006.

p. 50, "If they're missing . . . " Williams, *Eyes on the Prize*, 231.

p. 50, "Of course I . . . " Sally Belfrage, *Freedom Summer*, 126.

p. 50, "We posed as . . . " Keesecker, interview.

p. 51, "In my twenty-five . . . " McAdam, *Freedom Summer*, 155.

p. 51, "We won't be . . . " Wexler, *An Eyewitness History*, 211.

p. 51, "Our grief, though . . . " Obituary of Robert W. Goodman, *Time,* May 30, 1969, http://jcgi.pathfinder.com/time/magazine/article/0,9171,840139,00.html.

p. 53, "You could always . . . " Hargreaves, interview.

p. 53, "living in extreme . . . " Keesecker, interview.

p. 53, "The jobs above . . . " Williams, "Murder in Mississippi."

p. 54, "As we walked . . . " Michener, interview.

p. 54, "Most Mississippi blacks . . . " Hargreaves, interview.

p. 54, "There were loaded . . . " Williams, "Murder in Mississippi."

p. 54-55, "They opened their . . . " Booth, interview.

p. 55, "They were the . . . " Gloria Clark, interview with
author, September 10, 2006.

p. 55-56, "Every day I . . . " Mark Weiss, *Civil Rights
Movement
Veterans: Veterans Roll Call*, http://www.crmvet.org/
vet/weiss.htm.

p. 57, "You had to . . . " Gloria Clark, e-mail message to
Tom Davies (for dissertation research at Leeds University,
United Kingdom), April 4, 2005.

p. 57, "One time, a . . . " Than Porter, interview with
author, September 10, 2006.

p. 57, "It is the . . . " Mills, *Like a Holy Crusade*, 113.

p. 57-58, "All summer we . . . " Michener, interview.

p. 58, "But after Mississippi . . . " Hargreaves, interview.

p. 59, "The songs of . . . " Booth, interview.

p. 59, "The Mass Meetings . . . " Patti Miller's personal
Web site, "Mass Meetings," *Keeping History Alive*,
<http://www.keepinghistoryalive.com/bookexcerpts4.
html>.

CHAPTER SIX: Daring to Register

p. 60-61, "We approached, knocked . . . " Keesecker,
interview.

p. 62, "I work in . . . " McAdam, *Freedom Summer*, 79.

p. 62, "The whole house . . . " Ibid., 87.

p. 62, "The black professionals . . . " Cieciorka, interview.

p. 63, "Once in a . . . " Hargreaves, interview.

p. 64, "This is really . . . " Mills, *Like a Holy Crusade*, 132.

p. 64-65, "The county seat . . . " Elizabeth Sutherland
Martínez, ed., *Letters from Mississippi* (Brookline, Mass.:
Zephyr Press, 2002), 76.

p. 66, "There was less . . . " Mills, *Like a Holy Crusade*, 55.

p. 66, "I could not . . . " Ibid., 133.

p. 66-67, "[I]n 1964, county . . . " Michener, interview.

p. 67, "Fear reigned at . . . " Mills, *Like a Holy Crusade*, 138.

CHAPTER SEVEN: Freedom Schools

p. 68, "I was the . . . " Wilfred H. Stone, *Civil Rights Movement Veterans: Veterans Roll Call*, http://www.crmvet. org/ vet/stone.htm.

p. 69, "They told me . . . " Hargreaves, interview.

p. 69, "provide an educational . . . " Kathy Emery's official Web Site, "Democracy and Education: Memorandum to Freedom School Teachers," http://www. educationanddemocracy.org/FSCfiles/B_08 _MemoToFSTeachers.hm, (reprinted with permission of the King Library and Archives, The Martin Luther King Jr. Center for Nonviolence Social Change).

p. 70, "The students were . . . " Kathy Emery's official Web site, "Education and Democracy: Mississippi Freedom School Curriculum," http://www.educationanddemocracy. org/FSCfiles/B_16_FSchoolsInMSFusco.hm.

p. 71, "the kids were . . . " Deborah Rand, interview with author, September 9, 2006.

p. 71, "The atmosphere in . . . " Pam Parker, *Civil Rights Movement Veterans: Images*, "Mississippi Freedom Summer—1964," http://www.crmvet.org/images/imgfs. htm.

p. 72, "Some people think . . . " Ibid.

p. 72, "The children were . . . " Jo Ann Robinson, interview with author, September 16, 2006.

p. 72, "was so glad . . . " Porter, interview.

p. 72-73, "I just remember . . . " Clark, interview with Wilbur Colom.

p. 74, "I learned from . . . " Ibid.

CHAPTER EIGHT: The Freedom Party

p. 74, "if there's anybody . . . " Williams, *Eyes on the Prize*, 233.

p. 76, "'Joe, just give . . . " Ibid., 235.

p. 76, "We did not . . . " Wexler, *An Eyewitness History*, 213.

p. 78, "We are going . . . " Fannie Lou Hamer, Voices of Freedom Speech Archive, Web site of Professor Garth Pauley at Calvin College (original transcript courtesy of Lyndon Baines Johnson Presidential Library), http://www.calvin.edu/academic/cas/programs/pauley/voices/fhamer.htm.

p. 78, "The second Negro . . . " Ibid.

p. 78, "All of this . . . " Ibid.

p. 79, "You cannot trust . . . " Charlie Cobb, "Guinea: From Stokely Carmichael To Kwame Ture," *allafrica.com*, November 18, 1998, http://allafrica.com/stories/200101050369.html.

p. 81, "What would I . . . " Ibid.

CHAPTER NINE: Violence and Tension

p. 83, "I really cannot . . . " McAdam, *Freedom Summer*, 97.

p. 84, "Greenwood: Six local . . . " "Mississippi Summer Project—running summary of incidents: Transcript, August 12," Civil Rights in Mississippi Digital Archive, the University of Southern Mississippi, http://anna.lib.usm.edu/~spcol/crda/zwerling/mz054.html.

p. 84, ""I was beaten . . . " Cieciorka, interview.

p. 84, "If anyone isn't . . . " Hargreaves, interview.

p. 84-85, "And the carport . . . " McAdam, *Freedom Summer*, 90.

p. 85, "During a meeting . . . " Rand, interview.

p. 85, "I stayed in . . . " Spes Dolphin, interview with author, September 18, 2006.

p. 86, "Out in the . . . " Carson, *Civil Rights Chronicle*, 277.

p. 89, "not one single . . . " Hodding Carter, *The South Strikes Back* (Garden City, NY: Doubleday, 1959.), 137.

p. 89, "My grandmother was . . . " Wexler, *An Eyewitness History*, 211.

p. 89, "At a mass . . . " David Gass, interview with author, September 18, 2006.

p. 89, "Freedom! Freedom! . . . " Belfrage, *Freedom Summer*, 146.

p. 89, "frail old woman . . . " Ibid., 146-47.

p. 89-90, "Everyone experienced a . . . " Rand, interview.

p. 90, "Several times I've . . . " McAdam, *Freedom Summer*, 104.

p. 91, "was who took . . . " Michener, interview.

p. 91-92, "came to the rescue . . . " Ibid.

p. 92, "They had been . . . " Rand, interview.

p. 92, "There was interaction . . . " Carson, *Civil Rights Chronicle*, 269.

p. 92, "We shelled peas . . . " Michener, interview.

p. 93, "I had to . . . " Ibid.

p. 93, "[S]uddenly I'm back . . . " McAdam, *Freedom Summer*, 134.

CHAPTER TEN: The Impact of Freedom Summer

p. 95, "At Oberlin [College] . . . " Jerry Von Korff, *Civil Rights Movement Veterans: Veterans Roll Call,* July 19, 2001, http://www.crmvet.org/vet/korff.htm.

p. 96, "This Civil Rights . . . " Lyndon B. Johnson, "President Lyndon B. Johnson's Radio and Television Remarks Upon Signing the Civil Rights Bill," Lyndon Baines Johnson Library and Museum, http://www.lbjlib. utexas.edu/johnson/archives.hom/speeches.hom/ 640702.asp.

p. 97, "In order to . . . " Hargreaves, interview.

p. 98-99, "could not develop . . . " McAdam, *Freedom Summer*, 124.

p. 100, "If America don't . . . " Carson, *Civil Rights Chronicle*, 328.

p. 102, "Last summer I . . . " Ibid., 203.

p. 102, "no way he . . . " McAdam, *Freedom Summer*, 166.

p. 103, "The heroism I . . . " Gass, interview.

p. 104, "It was stunning . . . " Carson, *Civil Rights Chronicle*, 257.

p. 105, "A few became . . . " Steele, "Summer of Hate." 2004.

p. 106, "[I]f you organize . . . " Booth, interview.

p. 106, "Although I was . . . " Porter, interview.

p. 106, "After Freedom Summer . . . " Taylor, interview.

Bibliography

Adickes, Sandra E. *The Legacy of a Freedom School.* New York: Palgrave Macmillan, 2005.

Andrews, Kenneth T. *Freedom Is a Constant Struggle.* Chicago: University of Chicago Press, 2004.

Belfrage, Sally. *Freedom Summer.* Greenwich, Conn.: Fawcett Publications, 1965.

Branch, Taylor. *Pillar of Fire.* New York: Simon & Schuster, 1997.

Carson, Clayborne, David J. Garrow, Vincent Harding, and Darlene Clark Hine, eds. *Eyes on the Prize: A Reader and Guide.* New York: Penguin Books, 1987.

Carson, Clayborne, primary consultant. *Civil Rights Chronicle.* Lincolnwood, Ill.: Legacy Publishing, 2003.

Carter, Hodding. *The South Strikes Back.* Garden City, N.Y.: Doubleday, 1959.

Civil Rights Movement Veterans: John W. Hardy, Deborah Rand, Wilfred H. Stone, Jerry Von Korff, Mark Weiss. "Mississippi Freedom Summer—1964." The Civil Rights Movement Veterans' official Web site, http://www.crmvet.org/images/imgfs.htm.

Clark, Gloria. Interview with Wilbur Colom. Mississippi Oral History Program. McCaim Library and Archives, University of Southern Mississippi, December 12, 1995.

———. Clark. Interview with Tom Davies. Mississippi
Oral History Program. McCaim Library and
Archives, University of Southern Mississippi, April
4, 2005.

Cobb, Charlie. "Guinea: From Stokely Carmichael To
Kwame Ture," *Africa News Service*, November 18, 1998.
http://allafrica.com/stories/200101050369.html?page=3.

Cozzens, Lizza. "Mississippi & Freedom Summer." The
Web site of Robert N.M. Watson, http://www.watson.
org/~lisa/blackhistory/civilrights-55-65/missippi.html.

Currie, Stephen. *Murder in Mississippi.* Farmington
Hills, Mich.: Thomson Gale, 2006.

Emery, Kathy. "Democracy and Education: Memorandum
to Freedom School Teachers." http://www.educationandde
mocracy.org/FSCfiles/B_08_MemoToFSTeachers.htm.

Farber, David, primary consultant *The Sixties Chronicle*
Lincolnwood, Ill.: Legacy Publishing, 2004.

Hampton, Henry. *Voices of Freedom.* New York:
Bantam Books, 1990.

Holt, Len. *The Summer That Didn't End.* New York: Da
Capo Press.

Jaehnig, K.C. "Freedom Summer volunteer recounts tense times."
Southern Illinois University, February 5, 2002. http://
www.siu.edu/~anthro/adams/pages/news_service_fs.html.

Linder, Douglas O. "Bending Toward Justice: John Doar
and the Mississippi Burning Trial." *Mississippi Law
Journal* (Winter 2002). http://www.law.umkc.edu/
faculty/projects/ftrials/trialheroes/doaressay.html.

The Lyndon B. Johnson Library and Museum. "President
Lyndon B. Johnson's Radio and Television Remarks

Upon Signing the Civil Rights Bill." http://www.lbjlib.
utexas.edu/johnson/archives.hom/speeches.hom/
640702.asp.

Martínez, Elizabeth Sutherland, ed. *Letters from Mississippi.*
Brookline, Mass.: Zephyr Press, 2002.

McAdam, Doug. *Freedom Summer.* New York: Oxford
University Press, 1988.

———."Democracy and Education: Mississippi Freedom
School Curriculum." http://www.educationanddemocracy.
org/FSCfiles/B_08_MemoToFSTeachers.htm.

Miller, Patti. "Dirt." Patti Miller's personal Web site,
http://www.keepinghistoryalive.com/book-excerpts.html.

———. "Living with Dying." http://www.keepinghistoryalive.
com/book-excerpts3.html.

———. "Mass Meetings." http://www.keepinghistory
alive.com/book-excerpts3.html.

Mills, Nicolaus. *Like a Holy Crusade.* Chicago: Elephant
Paperbacks, 1993.

Moody, Anne. *Coming of Age in Mississippi.* New
York: Bantam: 1968.

Pauley, Garth. "Fannie Lou Hamer." Voices of Freedom
of Speech Archive. Official Web site of Garth Pauley
at Calvin College. http://www.calvin.edu/academic/cas/
programs/pauley/voices/fhamer.htm.

Steele, Jonathan. "Summer of Hate." *Guardian,* June 18,
2004. http://www.crmvet.org/nars/sohjs.htm.

Tusa, Bobs, and Herbert Randall. *Faces of Freedom
Summer.* Tuscaloosa, Alab.: University of Alabama
Press, 2001.

Wexler, Sanford. *An Eyewitness History to the Civil
Rights Movement.* New York: Checkmark Books, 1999.

Williams, Juan. *Eyes on the Prize.* New York: Penguin
    Books, 1987.
Woolley, John, and Gerhard Peters. "John F. Kennedy."
    The American Presidency Project, http://www.presidency.
    ucsb.edu/ws/index.php?pid=25966.

Web sites

http://www.americanradioworks.org/features/oh_freedom/
American RadioWorks correspondent John Biewen interviews Freedom Summer veterans in this excellent audio and print collection titled "Oh Freedom Over Me."

http://www.watson.org/~lisa/blackhistory/civilrights-55-65/missippi.html
Lisa Cozzens began building this site, *African American History*, in 1995 as a final project in her tenth grade African history class. The site is split into five sections, including one titled the "Civil Rights Movement 1955-1965: Mississippi and Freedom Summer." Here you'll find detailed information about Freedom Summer, along with links to an extensive bibliography.

http://www.spartacus.schoolnet.co.uk/USAfreedomS.htm
Spartacus Educational provides a succinct account of Freedom Summer, as well as some interesting side details, including newspaper editorials, a letter written by a student worker to his parents, and an application letter to join the movement from Rita Schwerner, whose husband, Michael, was shot dead on a rural road in Mississippi.

http://www.ibiblio.org/sncc/audio.html
Four graduates of the University of North Carolina, Chapel Hill, put together this Web site, which covers the Student Nonviolent Coordinating Committee from its birth in 1960 to 1966. Here, you can listen to Bob Moses, the architect of the voter registration drive in Mississippi, describe the Greenwood Voter Registration Project, as well as read a short biography of Fannie Lou Hamer, among other features.

Index